The Flavors of

BON APPÉTIT

2004

Blackberry Sorbet (page 223)

The Flavors of
BON APPÉTIT
2004

from the Editors of Bon Appétit

Condé Nast Books

New York

For *Bon Appétit* Magazine

Barbara Fairchild, *Editor-in-Chief*
Tricia Callas O'Donnell, *Contributing Editor, Books*
Marcy MacDonald, *Editorial Operations Director*
Carri Marks Oosterbaan, *Editorial Production Director*
Lynne Hartung, *Editorial Production Manager*
Sybil Shimazu Neubauer, *Editorial Administrator*
Marcia Hartmann Lewis, *Editorial Support*
Susan Champlin, *Text*
Shayna Sobol, *Copy Editor*
Gaylen Ducker Grody, *Research*
Elizabeth A. Matlin, *Index*

For Condé Nast Books

Lisa Faith Phillips, *Vice President and General Manager*
Tom Downing, *Direct Marketing Director*
Deborah Williams, *Operations Director*
Lyn Barris Hastings, *Senior Project Manager*
Fianna Reznik, *Direct Marketing Associate*
Eric Levy, *Inventory Associate*
Eric Killer, *Project Associate*

Design: Monica Elias and Ph.D

Front Jacket: Smothered Grilled Pork Chops (page 69) and Grilled Corn Salad with Lima Beans and Tomatoes (page 160)
Facing Page: Top: Zucchini and Spinach Soup (page 33)
Middle: Barbecued Rack of Lamb with Tomato-Mint Dressing (page 58)
Bottom: Triple-Layer White Cake with Orange Curd Filling and Frosting (page 206)

Published by Condé Nast Books, Random House Direct, Inc., New York, New York.
A wholly owned subsidiary of Random House, Inc.

Printed in the United States of America

Library of Congress Cataloging-in-Publication Data is available upon request.

10 9 8 7 6 5 4 3 2 1

FIRST EDITION

Condé Nast Web Address: bonappetit.com
Bon Appétit Books Web Address: bonappetitbooks.com

Contents

Introduction

It's late Sunday afternoon, and you're in the mood for a really good burger. Because you're an enthusiastic cook, you want to make this burger yourself. And because you're a *Bon Appétit* reader, you're looking for something both familiar and fantastic, something that has all the comfort of a traditional burger but with a sophisticated twist. The answer: a Napa Valley Cabernet Burger. This delicious recipe (you can find it on page 45) blends easy-to-find ingredients—like ground beef, fresh rosemary, cheddar cheese, and a bottle of Cabernet Sauvignon—into something at once brand-new and tried-and-true.

This is what *Bon Appétit* does best: creating recipes that combine your favorite ingredients in exciting and completely contemporary ways. Recipes that motivate, inspire, and reward the home cook. Recipes you can count on for foolproof results.

At *Bon Appétit*, we're keenly aware of the way people like to cook and eat. We know—because you tell us, and because we feel exactly the same way—that you like casual entertaining (but that you're ready to pull out all the stops when the occasion is right). You like meals that can be prepared quickly (but taste as if you slaved over them for hours). That you're eager to try all kinds of ethnic cuisines and ingredients (but that "Italian" always tops the list in our annual March survey). And that sometimes, nothing else will do but a good old-fashioned layer cake or hearty macaroni and cheese.

We also pay close attention to the ingredients and dishes that have been causing a stir, so to

Napa Valley Cabernet Burgers (page 45)

speak, over the course of the year. We cruise the farmers' markets, we sample every kind of restaurant (poor us!), and we watch what's being snapped up in the supermarkets, ethnic markets, and specialty foods stores. And we incorporate these influences into delicious recipes that fit naturally into our real lives.

In this book—a collection of the best *Bon Appétit* recipes of the past year—you'll find the flavors and ingredients that are at the forefront of the culinary world. Here are the succulent short ribs, those gorgeous fresh vegetables from the farmers' market, that wild Alaskan salmon, all presented to their best advantage in Beef Short Ribs in Chipotle and Green Chili Sauce (page 52); Cider-Glazed Root Vegetables (page 139); and Miso-Marinated Salmon with Cucumber-Daikon Relish (page 94).

Fresh Blueberry Tart (page 176)

You'll also find the foods and ingredients you've consistently told us are among your favorites—such as Mexican cuisine, Parmesan cheese, and all manner of irresistible desserts. You'll discover them in recipes like Chicken in Green Pumpkin Seed Sauce (page 78); Pizza Bianca with Prosciutto, Arugula, and Parmesan (page 134); and Triple-Chocolate Pudding Pie with Cappuccino Cream (page 178).

At *Bon Appétit,* we understand exactly what it means to be in the mood for a really good burger—or a great pasta dish or a fresh blueberry tart. In fact, being rather enthusiastic eaters ourselves, we know all about food moods. And in *The Flavors of Bon Appétit 2004,* you'll find recipes to satisfy every single one.

Onion and Bacon Tart (page 23)

Starters

Appetizers

Soups

Beverages

Curried Wild Mushroom Pâté

 5 tablespoons butter
1¼ pounds fresh shiitake mushrooms, stemmed, or crimini mushrooms, very coarsely chopped
 ½ cup chopped shallots (about 2 large)
 2 garlic cloves, chopped
1¾ teaspoons curry powder
 ½ teaspoon ground cumin

 1 cup roasted salted cashews
 2 tablespoons olive oil
 2 tablespoons finely chopped mixed fresh herbs (such as parsley, chives, and basil)

   Fresh parsley or basil sprigs (optional)
 1 French-bread baguette, cut into ½-inch-thick slices, toasted

Melt butter in heavy large skillet over medium-high heat. Add mushrooms, shallots, garlic, curry, and cumin and cook until mixture begins to brown and all liquid evaporates, stirring frequently, about 12 minutes. Cool.

Using on/off turns, finely chop cashews in processor. Add oil and blend to coarse paste. Add mushroom mixture and chopped herbs; blend in using on/off turns until mushrooms are coarsely chopped. Season with salt and pepper.

Spoon pâté into bowl. Cover and chill 4 hours. (*Can be made 3 days ahead; keep chilled.*) Garnish pâté with herb sprigs, if desired. Serve with toasts.

10 SERVINGS

Creamy White Bean Dip

 1 15-ounce can cannellini (white kidney beans), drained
1½ tablespoons fresh lemon juice
1½ tablespoons extra-virgin olive oil
 1 large garlic clove, peeled
 ¾ teaspoon ground cumin
 1 tablespoon chopped fresh mint
 1 tablespoon chopped fresh dill
 1 teaspoon grated lemon peel
   Crudités (such as carrots, celery, and bell pepper)

Puree first 5 ingredients in processor until almost smooth. Season with salt and pepper. Transfer dip to small bowl. (*Can be prepared 1 day ahead. Cover and refrigerate.*) Mix mint, dill, and lemon peel in small dish; sprinkle over dip. Serve with crudités.

MAKES ABOUT 1¼ CUPS

Herbed Crab Cakes

½ cup mayonnaise
½ cup chopped fresh chives
¼ cup chopped fresh parsley
2 tablespoons fresh lemon juice
1 teaspoon Old Bay seasoning or other seafood seasoning blend
¼ teaspoon cayenne pepper
1¾ pounds lump crabmeat, picked over
5 cups fresh breadcrumbs made from crustless French bread

3 tablespoons butter
3 tablespoons olive oil
Lemon wedges

These are perfect for a party: They can be prepared up to six hours ahead and they cook up quickly.

Mix first 6 ingredients in large bowl. Stir in crab. Add 2 cups breadcrumbs; mix well. Season with black pepper.

Place remaining 3 cups breadcrumbs in medium bowl. Using scant ¼ cupful for each, shape crab mixture into patties. Drop into breadcrumbs; turn to coat, pressing crumbs to adhere. Arrange cakes on baking sheet. (*Can be made 6 hours ahead. Cover; chill.*)

Melt half of butter and half of oil in heavy large skillet over medium-high heat. Add half of crab cakes. Sauté until heated through and golden brown, about 5 minutes per side. Arrange on platter. Repeat with remaining butter, oil, and crab cakes. Garnish with lemon.

MAKES 20

Shrimp Risotto with Spinach and Basil

  6 cups (about) low-salt chicken broth
  1 pound uncooked large shrimp, peeled, deveined

  2 tablespoons olive oil
1½ cups chopped onion
  2 large garlic cloves, minced
1½ cups arborio rice or medium-grain white rice (about 9½ ounces)
  ½ cup dry white wine
  1 6-ounce package baby spinach leaves
  ½ cup freshly grated Parmesan cheese, plus additional for passing
  ¼ cup chopped fresh basil

Bring 6 cups broth to simmer in medium saucepan. Add shrimp. Turn off heat, cover, and let stand until shrimp are just opaque in center, about 3 minutes. Using slotted spoon, transfer shrimp to small bowl; cover with foil to keep warm. Cover broth to keep warm.

Heat oil in heavy large saucepan over medium heat. Add onion; sauté until tender, about 5 minutes. Add garlic; stir 1 minute. Add rice; stir until edge of rice is translucent but center is still opaque, about 2 minutes. Add wine; cook until absorbed, stirring occasionally, about 2 minutes. Add ¾ cup broth. Simmer until almost all broth is absorbed, stirring often, about 2 minutes. Continue to add broth, ¾ cup at a time, until rice is just tender and mixture is creamy, stirring often and allowing almost all broth to be absorbed after each addition, about 25 minutes total. During last 5 minutes, add spinach in 4 batches, stirring and allowing spinach to wilt after each addition. Mix in shrimp, ½ cup cheese, and basil. Season with salt and pepper. Spoon risotto into shallow bowls and serve, passing additional cheese separately.

6 SERVINGS

Roasted Red Pepper, Almond, and Garlic Dip

  ½ cup whole natural almonds (about 3 ounces), toasted
  1 cup drained roasted red bell peppers from jar
  2 teaspoons red wine vinegar
  1 large garlic clove, peeled
  2 tablespoons extra-virgin olive oil
    Pita chips

Very finely chop almonds in processor. Add peppers, vinegar, and garlic; process to coarse puree. With machine running, pour oil through feed tube and process until puree thickens slightly. Season with salt and pepper. Transfer to small bowl. (*Dip can be made 1 day ahead. Cover; chill. Bring to room temperature before serving.*) Serve with pita chips.

MAKES ABOUT 1¼ CUPS

Spicy Baby Okra and Olives

12 ounces fresh baby okra or small okra
¼ cup halved pitted Kalamata olives
¼ cup halved pitted cracked green olives
¼ cup pimiento-stuffed green olives
½ cup fresh lemon juice
½ cup extra-virgin olive oil
3 tablespoons fresh thyme leaves
2 garlic cloves, thinly sliced
½ teaspoon coarse kosher salt
½ teaspoon dried crushed red pepper

Combine okra and all olives in 1-quart resealable plastic bag. Whisk lemon juice and all remaining ingredients in medium bowl to blend. Pour marinade over okra and olives; seal bag. Turn bag to distribute marinade evenly. Refrigerate at least 1 day and up to 2 days, turning occasionally.

12 SERVINGS

Breadsticks with Prosciutto and Arugula

Butter, room temperature
12 10- to 12-inch-long grissini or other long
    thin breadsticks
⅓ cup freshly grated Parmesan cheese
12 4x3-inch thin prosciutto slices
60 arugula leaves (about 2 large bunches)

Spread some butter over 4 inches of 1 end of each breadstick. Spread Parmesan cheese on plate. Roll buttered end of each breadstick in cheese to coat lightly. Place 1 slice prosciutto on work surface; arrange 3 arugula leaves atop prosciutto, then place cheese-covered end of breadstick atop arugula and roll up prosciutto around breadstick, enclosing arugula. Repeat procedure with remaining breadsticks. *(Can be prepared 2 hours ahead. Place breadsticks in tall glass, prosciutto ends up. Cover with plastic wrap and chill.)* Tuck 2 arugula leaves into prosciutto end of each breadstick and serve.

MAKES 12

Beet Carpaccio with Goat Cheese and Mint Vinaigrette

12   2-inch beets, trimmed

1   cup crumbled soft fresh goat cheese (about 5 ounces)

2   tablespoons minced shallot

⅓   cup unseasoned rice vinegar

⅓   cup chopped fresh mint

¼   cup walnut oil or olive oil

1½   teaspoons sugar

¼   cup chopped fresh chives

Thinly sliced beets (not beef) lay the foundation for this vibrant rendition of the Italian appetizer. Use any assortment of small beets—red, golden, purple, or candy-striped. A local farmers' market will have the best selection. The beets can be roasted and peeled one day before serving.

Preheat oven to 350°F. Line rimmed baking sheet with foil. Place beets on sheet (if using both light- and dark-colored beets, place them on separate sheets to prevent discoloration). Sprinkle beets lightly with water. Cover tightly with foil. Bake until beets are tender when pierced with fork, about 40 minutes. Cool on sheet. Peel beets. (*Can be prepared 1 day ahead. Place in resealable plastic bag; chill.*)

Using cheese slicer or knife, slice beets very thinly. Slightly overlap slices on 6 plates, dividing equally. Sprinkle with cheese, then shallot, salt, and pepper. Whisk vinegar, mint, oil, and sugar in small bowl. Season with salt and pepper. Drizzle over beets. Sprinkle with chives.

6 SERVINGS

Brie and Walnut Quesadillas with Tropical Fruit Salsa

SALSA

- 1 cup ⅓-inch dice peeled cored pineapple
- 1 cup ⅓-inch dice peeled pitted mango
- 1 cup ⅓-inch dice peeled seeded papaya
- ½ cup ⅓-inch dice red bell pepper
- ¼ cup chopped fresh cilantro
- 2 tablespoons fresh lime juice
- 1 serrano chile, minced, with seeds

QUESADILLAS

- Butter, room temperature
- 8 8-inch-diameter flour tortillas
- 1 pound chilled Brie, rind trimmed, cut into ½-inch-thick slices
- 24 fresh cilantro sprigs
- 1 cup Candied Maple Walnuts (see recipe below)

FOR SALSA: Toss all ingredients in large bowl. Season with salt and pepper. (*Can be made 3 hours ahead. Cover; chill.*)

FOR QUESADILLAS: Butter tortillas on 1 side; place, buttered side down, on large rimmed baking sheet. Top half of each tortilla with cheese, cilantro sprigs, and nuts. Fold tortillas in half; press lightly. (*Can be made 1 day ahead. Cover; chill.*)

Preheat oven to 300°F. Working in batches, cook tortillas in heavy large skillet over medium heat until golden and cheese melts, about 1 minute per side. Transfer to baking sheet. Keep warm in oven. Cut each into 3 wedges. Serve with salsa.

10 SERVINGS

Candied Maple Walnuts

- 1 cup walnut halves
- 2 tablespoons pure maple syrup

Preheat oven to 300°F. Line rimmed baking sheet with foil. Combine walnuts and maple syrup in medium bowl; toss to coat. Spread out nuts on sheet. Bake until browned and dry, stirring often, about 22 minutes. Cool. Remove from foil. Coarsely chop nuts. (*Can be made 3 days ahead. Store airtight at room temperature.*)

MAKES 1 CUP

Indian-Spiced Chicken Kebabs with Cilantro Chutney

CILANTRO CHUTNEY

- ½ cup (packed) fresh mint leaves
- ½ cup (packed) fresh cilantro leaves
- 1 tablespoon fresh lemon juice
- 2½ teaspoons minced fresh ginger
- 1 jalapeño chile, seeded, minced
- 2 tablespoons (or more) plain yogurt

CHICKEN

- ½ cup plain yogurt
- 3 tablespoons tikka paste or mild curry paste (such as Patak's)
- 1 tablespoon olive oil
- 2 garlic cloves, minced
- 2 teaspoons minced fresh ginger
- ¼ teaspoon cayenne pepper
- 1½ pounds skinless boneless chicken breasts, cut into 2-inch cubes

- 24 (about) 6-inch bamboo skewers, soaked 30 minutes in water
  Butter lettuce leaves
- ½ small English hothouse cucumber, halved lengthwise, thinly sliced crosswise
- 2 limes, cut into wedges

Tikka curry paste—used to season the chicken—can be found in Asian markets, but any mild Indian curry paste can be substituted.

FOR CHUTNEY: Blend first 5 ingredients and 2 tablespoons yogurt in blender or processor. Blend in more yogurt if necessary to make smooth paste. (*Chutney can be made 1 day ahead. Cover and refrigerate.*)

FOR CHICKEN: Whisk first 6 ingredients in large bowl to blend. Add chicken; toss to coat. Cover; refrigerate at least 2 hours and up to 12 hours.

Preheat broiler. Thread 1 chicken piece on each skewer. Cover exposed part of skewers with foil. Broil chicken until cooked through, turning occasionally, about 8 minutes. Arrange lettuce and cucumber on platter. Top with chicken. Squeeze lime over. Serve chicken with cilantro chutney.

MAKES ABOUT 24

Toasted Garbanzo Beans and Pistachios with Cumin and Cayenne

2 15½-ounce cans garbanzo beans (chickpeas), drained
¼ cup corn oil
1 teaspoon coarse sea salt
1 teaspoon ground cumin
1 teaspoon ground black pepper
½ teaspoon cayenne pepper

1 cup shelled raw pistachios
2 teaspoons fresh thyme leaves

Preheat oven to 400°F. Toss garbanzo beans with next 5 ingredients in medium bowl. Transfer mixture to rimmed baking sheet. Bake until garbanzos are golden and crisp, stirring occasionally with metal spatula, about 20 minutes. *(Can be made 4 hours ahead. Keep at room temperature.)*

Stir pistachios and thyme into garbanzo mixture. Bake until beans and pistachios are crunchy, about 12 minutes. Transfer mixture to bowl and serve warm.

MAKES 2½ CUPS

This simple recipe is a sensational addition to a classic cheese platter.

Baguettes with Smoked Salmon and Dill Butter

6 tablespoons unsalted European-style butter, room temperature
1 tablespoon chopped fresh dill
1 tablespoon drained capers

½ French-bread baguette
   Dijon mustard
1 cup watercress, thick stems trimmed
6 ounces smoked salmon
   Coarsely ground black pepper

Mix first 3 ingredients in small bowl.

Cut baguette horizontally in half. Spread Dijon mustard on cut sides of bread. Spread dill butter over. Top with watercress, then smoked salmon. Sprinkle with pepper. Cut each sandwich crosswise into 6 equal pieces, making 12 total.

MAKES 12

European-style butter—rich, higher-fat butter long favored on the Continent but rarely served in the United States—is increasingly easier to find on our shores.

Fried Mozzarella with
Anchovy, Caper, and Garlic Sauce

2 8-ounce balls fresh water-packed mozzarella cheese, drained, each cut into four rounds
   All purpose flour
1 large egg, beaten to blend
3 cups fresh breadcrumbs made from crustless French bread (about 8 ounces)

2 tablespoons (¼ stick) butter
6 garlic cloves, minced
1 cup (packed) fresh Italian parsley
½ cup olive oil
⅓ cup drained capers
1 2-ounce can anchovy fillets, drained
1½ teaspoons fresh lemon juice

Coat cheese in flour, then egg, then breadcrumbs. Place on baking sheet. Cover and refrigerate until cold, at least 2 hours.

Meanwhile, melt butter in small skillet over low heat. Add garlic; sauté about 3 minutes. Transfer to processor. Add parsley, ¼ cup oil, capers, anchovies, and lemon juice. Blend until coarse paste forms. Season with salt and pepper. *(Cheese and sauce can be made 1 day ahead. Cover separately; chill. Rewarm sauce slightly over low heat before serving.)*

Heat ¼ cup oil in large skillet over high heat. Working in batches, fry cheese until brown, about 2 minutes per side.

Transfer fried cheese to plates. Spoon warm sauce over cheese.

8 SERVINGS

Jade Dumplings with Soy-Sesame Dipping Sauce

DIPPING SAUCE
⅓ cup soy sauce
1 green onion, very thinly sliced
2 tablespoons rice vinegar
2 teaspoons oriental sesame oil

DUMPLINGS
1 tablespoon minced fresh ginger
1 garlic clove, peeled
12 ounces fresh asparagus, trimmed, quartered crosswise
1 8-ounce can whole water chestnuts, drained
3 green onions, quartered
1 teaspoon oriental sesame oil

The dumplings can be assembled and chilled up to eight hours before steaming.

1 teaspoon soy sauce

¼ teaspoon coarse kosher salt

All purpose flour

36 wonton wrappers

Romaine lettuce leaves

FOR DIPPING SAUCE: Stir all ingredients in small bowl to blend.

FOR DUMPLINGS: Finely mince ginger and garlic in food processor. Add asparagus and next 5 ingredients; using on/off turns, process filling until asparagus is finely chopped but not pureed.

Sprinkle baking sheet with flour. Place 1 wonton wrapper on work surface. Spoon 2 teaspoons filling into center. Moisten edges of wrapper with water; gather corners together over filling. Twist edges together, enclosing filling completely. Place on baking sheet. Repeat with remaining wrappers and filling. (*Sauce and dumplings can be made 8 hours ahead. Cover separately and chill.*)

Place steamer rack in large pot. Pour enough water into pot to reach depth of ½ inch. Line rack with lettuce. Bring water to simmer. Working in batches, arrange dumplings side by side (but not touching) on rack. Cover; steam 15 minutes. Serve dumplings with dipping sauce.

MAKES 36

Goat Cheese in Grape Leaves with Tomato and Olive Salad

½ cup olive oil
4 teaspoons chopped fresh thyme
¾ teaspoon coarsely ground black pepper
12 large grape leaves from jar, rinsed, patted dry, stemmed
3 4- to 5-ounce logs soft fresh goat cheese, each cut crosswise into 4 rounds

¼ cup extra-virgin olive oil
2 tablespoons balsamic vinegar
2 teaspoons Dijon mustard
6 large tomatoes, thinly sliced
⅓ cup coarsely chopped pitted oil-cured black olives (about 30)

6 ½-inch-thick slices crusty country-style white bread

Whisk ½ cup oil, thyme, and pepper in small bowl to blend. Arrange grape leaves, vein side up, on work surface. Dip each cheese round into oil and place in center of 1 grape leaf. Fold sides of leaves over cheese; fold up bottom and continue to roll up, enclosing cheese completely. Arrange seam side down on platter. Brush lightly with oil. Cover; chill 1 hour. *(Can be made 1 day ahead; keep chilled. Cover remaining oil and store at room temperature.)*

Prepare barbecue (medium-high heat). Whisk ¼ cup extra-virgin oil, vinegar, and mustard in small bowl to blend. Season with salt and pepper. Overlap tomato slices on platter. Drizzle with dressing; sprinkle with half of olives.

Place wrapped cheese rounds on grill, seam side down. Grill until cheese softens and leaves begin to char, about 2 minutes per side. Arrange cheeses atop tomatoes. Sprinkle with remaining olives.

Brush bread slices with remaining thyme oil. Grill bread until beginning to brown, turning occasionally, about 5 minutes. Cut toasts diagonally in half. Serve cheese, passing toasts separately.

12 SERVINGS

Onion and Bacon Tart

2¼ cups (or more) all purpose flour
1 cup warm water (110°F to 115°F)
1 teaspoon active dry yeast
½ teaspoon fine sea salt

¾ cup crème fraîche*
⅓ cup large-curd cottage cheese
⅓ cup sour cream
2 small white onions, very thinly sliced (about 1½ cups)
12 ounces ¼-inch-thick bacon slices cut crosswise into ½-inch-wide strips

   Freshly ground black pepper

Combine 1 cup flour, 1 cup warm water, and yeast in large bowl; stir to blend well. Cover bowl with plastic; let stand until mixture bubbles, about 30 minutes. Stir in salt, then 1¼ cups flour. Mix until soft slightly sticky dough forms, adding more flour by tablespoonfuls if very sticky. Cover bowl with plastic. Let rise in warm draft-free area until doubled, about 1½ hours.

Preheat oven to 500°F. Lightly flour 2 large baking sheets. Lightly flour hands; punch down dough and divide in half. Roll out each half on lightly floured surface to thin 16x10-inch rectangle. Transfer each to baking sheet. If dough shrinks, roll or stretch each back to size. Puree crème fraîche, cottage cheese, and sour cream in processor until smooth. Season with salt and pepper. Spread cream mixture over crusts. Sprinkle onions and raw bacon over, dividing equally. Bake until edges of crusts are crisp and brown, about 14 minutes. Sprinkle generously with pepper and serve.

Sold at some supermarkets. If unavailable, heat 1 cup whipping cream to lukewarm (85°F). Remove from heat and mix in 2 tablespoons buttermilk. Cover and let stand in warm, draft-free area until slightly thickened, 24 to 48 hours, depending on temperature of room. Refrigerate until ready to use.

6 SERVINGS

Mediterranean Dinner from the Grill for 8

Goat Cheese in Grape Leaves with Tomato and Olive Salad
(opposite)

Tuna Steaks with Herbed Aioli
(page 88; double recipe)

Sicilian Fennel and Orange Salad with Red Onion and Mint
(page 155; double recipe)

Grilled Vegetables

Pinot Grigio

Marsala and Dried-Fig Crostata
(page 182)

Cream of Cauliflower Soup with Saffron

 2 cups water
 2 cups low-salt chicken broth
 1/8 teaspoon coarsely crumbled saffron threads

 3 tablespoons butter
 2 cups chopped onions
 1 1/2 pounds cauliflower, cut into 1/2- to 3/4-inch pieces

 3/4 cup half and half
   Thinly sliced fresh chives

Combine 2 cups water and 2 cups low-salt chicken broth in medium saucepan. Bring mixture just to simmer. Remove from heat. Add saffron threads. Cover and steep 20 minutes.

Melt 3 tablespoons butter in heavy medium pot over medium-low heat. Add chopped onions and sauté until very tender but not brown, about 10 minutes. Add cauliflower pieces; stir to coat. Add saffron broth. Bring to simmer over high heat. Reduce heat, cover, and simmer until cauliflower pieces are tender, about 20 minutes.

Working in batches, puree cauliflower mixture in food processor until smooth. Transfer cauliflower puree to large saucepan. Stir in half and half and bring to simmer. Season to taste with salt and pepper. *(Can be made 1 day ahead. Cover and refrigerate. Bring to simmer before serving.)* Ladle soup into bowls. Garnish with sliced fresh chives and serve.

6 SERVINGS

Cilantro and Almond Soup

 6 1/2 cups (or more) low-salt chicken broth
 4 cups (packed) fresh cilantro
 2 cups (packed) fresh Italian parsley
 6 ounces cream cheese, cubed
 1/2 cup slivered almonds, toasted
 1 fresh marjoram sprig

Combine 2 cups broth, 2 cups cilantro, parsley, cream cheese, and almonds in blender; blend until smooth. Heat 4 1/2 cups broth in large saucepan. Whisk in herb-cheese mixture and marjoram. Simmer 25 minutes to blend flavors. Transfer 1 cup soup and remaining 2 cups cilantro to blender; puree until smooth. Add puree to soup in pan. Season with salt and pepper. Bring soup to simmer, thinning with more broth if desired.

4 TO 6 SERVINGS

Cannellini Soup with Parmesan Cheese

3 tablespoons extra-virgin olive oil plus additional oil for garnish
1 large onion, finely chopped (about 2 cups)
1 large carrot, finely chopped (about 1 cup)
1 large celery stalk, finely chopped (about ⅔ cup)
3 15-ounce cans cannellini (white kidney beans), drained
6 cups low-salt chicken broth
2 teaspoons minced fresh sage
2 2x2-inch Parmesan cheese rinds
3 ounces thinly sliced prosciutto, chopped

Freshly grated Parmesan cheese

Heat 3 tablespoons oil in heavy large pot over medium heat. Add onion, carrot, and celery and sauté until vegetables are soft, about 10 minutes. Add beans, broth, sage, Parmesan rinds, and prosciutto; simmer over medium-low heat, stirring occasionally, until flavors blend and soup thickens slightly, about 40 minutes. Using tongs, remove cheese rinds.

Puree about 5 cups soup in processor and return to pot. Season with salt and pepper. *(Soup can be made 2 days ahead. Refrigerate uncovered until cold, then cover and keep refrigerated. Rewarm before serving.)* Ladle soup into bowls and serve, passing grated Parmesan cheese and additional olive oil separately.

6 TO 8 SERVINGS

Beet and Cabbage Soup

¼ cup (½ stick) unsalted butter
3 cups coarsely chopped peeled raw beets (from 1½ pounds)
2 cups chopped red onions
3 celery stalks, coarsely chopped
1 cup chopped red cabbage
3 tablespoons finely chopped seeded jalapeño chiles
5 cups (or more) low-salt chicken broth
2 tablespoons fresh lime juice

   Sour cream

When beets are cooked as they are in this recipe, they turn a bright fuchsia color. Wear disposable plastic gloves when working with beets. Puree only one or two cups of hot soup at a time, holding the top of the blender firmly to keep it from flying off.

Melt butter in heavy large saucepan over medium-high heat. Add beets, onions, celery, cabbage, and chiles; sauté until celery is soft, about 10 minutes. Add 5 cups broth and lime juice; bring to boil. Reduce heat to medium-low. Cover and simmer until vegetables are very tender, about 1 hour 15 minutes.

Working in small batches, puree soup in blender. Return soup to pot; season with salt and pepper. Thin with more broth by ¼ cupfuls, if desired. Ladle into bowls; top with sour cream.

6 SERVINGS

Curried Butternut Squash Soup

2 tablespoons olive oil
2 cups chopped onions
1½ teaspoons curry powder
⅛ to ¼ teaspoon cayenne pepper
6 cups ½- to ¾-inch cubes peeled butternut squash (from 3 pounds)
3½ cups low-salt chicken broth
   Plain yogurt
   Fresh cilantro leaves

Heat oil in large pot over medium heat. Add onions. Cover; sauté until soft, about 5 minutes. Add curry powder and ⅛ teaspoon cayenne; stir 30 seconds. Add squash and broth; bring to boil. Reduce heat to medium-low. Cover; simmer until squash is very tender, about 30 minutes. Puree soup in batches in blender. Return to pot. Season with salt and pepper, adding more cayenne if desired. (*Can be made 1 day ahead. Chill uncovered until cold, then cover and keep chilled. Rewarm before serving.*) Ladle soup into bowls; top with dollop of yogurt and cilantro.

6 SERVINGS

Hominy, Tomato, and Chile Soup

1 teaspoon cumin seeds

2 tablespoons olive oil

1 cup finely chopped white onion

1 large fresh Anaheim chile,* stemmed, seeded, chopped (about ½ cup)

2 garlic cloves, minced

1 dried New Mexico chile,** stemmed, seeded, torn into small pieces

1 teaspoon dried oregano

4 cups low-salt chicken broth

1 14- to 15-ounce can golden hominy, drained

1 14- to 15-ounce can diced tomatoes in juice

⅓ cup finely crushed tostadas caseras or corn chips

1 to 2 tablespoons fresh lime juice

Tostadas *caseras*—corn tortillas that have been seasoned and fried—can be found with the tortillas in most supermarkets. The soup can be made one day before serving.

Toast cumin seeds in heavy small saucepan over medium heat until beginning to darken in color, stirring often, about 3 minutes. Cool 10 minutes. Enclose in plastic bag and crush with hammer or mallet.

Heat oil in heavy large saucepan over medium-high heat. Add onion, Anaheim chile, and garlic. Sauté until onion is translucent, about 5 minutes. Add New Mexico chile, oregano, and cumin seeds. Stir 2 minutes longer. Add broth, hominy, tomatoes with juices, and tostadas caseras. Bring soup to boil; reduce heat to medium-low, cover, and simmer until dried chile is very soft and flavors blend, about 45 minutes. Season soup with salt and pepper, then lime juice to taste. *(Can be made 1 day ahead. Chill uncovered until cold, then cover and keep chilled. Rewarm soup before serving.)* Ladle soup into bowls.

Also known as a California chile; available at Latin American markets and many supermarkets.
**Available at Latin American markets and some supermarkets.*

6 SERVINGS

Parsnip and Apple Soup

3 tablespoons butter

3 large leeks; white and pale green parts finely chopped, dark green parts reserved

5 large parsnips (about 1½ pounds), peeled, cut into ½-inch pieces

2 medium Gala or Fuji apples (about 13 ounces total), peeled, cored, cut into ½-inch pieces

4 cups (or more) water

1½ cups whole milk
   Large pinch of sugar

Melt butter in heavy large pot over medium-high heat. Add leeks, parsnips, and apples. Cover; cook until apples and vegetables begin to soften, stirring often, about 20 minutes. Add 4 cups water. Bring to boil. Reduce heat to medium. Simmer uncovered until apples and vegetables are very tender, about 20 minutes. Cool slightly.

Working in batches, puree apple-vegetable mixture with milk in blender until smooth, thinning soup with more water if desired. Return soup to pot. Season soup with sugar, salt, and pepper. (*Can be made 1 day ahead. Cool slightly. Refrigerate uncovered until cold, then cover and keep refrigerated.*)

Cut enough reserved dark green parts of leeks into matchstick-size strips to measure 1 cup. Cook in medium saucepan of boiling water until tender, about 10 minutes. Drain.

Bring soup to simmer. Ladle into bowls. Garnish with leek strips and serve.

6 SERVINGS

Carrot Soup with Sesame Seeds and Chives

5 tablespoons butter

3½ cups chopped peeled carrots

1 cup chopped leeks (white and pale green parts only)

½ cup chopped celery

6 cups low-salt chicken broth

½ cup whipping cream

½ cup sour cream

1 teaspoon oriental sesame oil

2 cups ½-inch bread cubes (from day-old crustless French bread)

1½ tablespoons sesame seeds, toasted

2 tablespoons chopped fresh chives

Melt 2 tablespoons butter in heavy large pot over medium heat. Add carrots, leeks, and celery. Cover and cook until vegetables soften slightly, stirring occasionally, about 10 minutes. Add broth; bring to boil. Reduce heat, cover, and simmer until vegetables are very tender, about 25 minutes. Cool slightly.

Working in batches, puree soup in blender until smooth. Return soup to pot. Whisk cream, sour cream, and ½ teaspoon sesame oil into soup. Season soup to taste with salt and pepper. *(Can be made 1 day ahead. Cover and chill.)*

Melt remaining 3 tablespoons butter with remaining ½ teaspoon sesame oil in heavy large skillet over medium heat. Add bread cubes and sauté until golden brown and crispy, about 4 minutes.

Bring soup almost to simmer over medium heat. Ladle into bowls. Mound croutons in center of each. Sprinkle with sesame seeds and chives and serve.

6 SERVINGS

Gazpacho with Herbs and Jalapeño

4 cups tomato juice

1 red onion, finely chopped (about 2 cups)

1 cucumber, halved, peeled, seeded, finely chopped (about 1½ cups)

1 red bell pepper, finely chopped (about 1 cup)

1 yellow bell pepper, finely chopped (about 1 cup)

2 tomatoes, seeded, finely chopped (about 1 cup)

¼ cup Champagne vinegar or white wine vinegar

1½ tablespoons chopped seeded jalapeño chile

1 tablespoon chopped fresh basil

1 tablespoon chopped fresh cilantro

1 tablespoon chopped fresh parsley

1 garlic clove, minced

¾ teaspoon hot pepper sauce

½ teaspoon salt

¼ teaspoon ground black pepper

Mix all ingredients in large bowl. Cover and chill until cold, at least 2 hours. *(Can be made 2 days ahead. Keep refrigerated.)*

8 SERVINGS

Saturday Night Dinner for 6

Parsnip and Apple Soup
(opposite)

Lemon-Parsley Veal Chops
(page 54)

Roasted Sugar Snap Peas with Fleur de Sel
(page 138)

Rice Pilaf

Vernaccia

Bittersweet Molten Chocolate Cakes with Coffee Ice Cream
(page 199)

Coffee and *Cognac*

Double Celery Soup

    2 tablespoons (¼ stick) butter
    1 tablespoon olive oil
    2 large leeks (white and pale green parts only), thinly sliced (about 2 cups)
    1 large onion, chopped
    2 medium-size Yukon Gold potatoes (about 12 ounces), peeled, cut into 1-inch cubes
    2 medium celery roots (celeriac; about 1½ pounds total), peeled, cut into ½-inch cubes
    2 large fresh thyme sprigs
    1 bay leaf
    8 cups low-salt chicken broth
    5 celery stalks with leaves, stalks thinly sliced, leaves reserved

    ⅓ cup whipping cream

Melt butter with oil in heavy large pot over medium heat. Add leeks and onion and sauté until almost tender, about 10 minutes. Stir in potatoes, celery roots, thyme, and bay leaf. Add broth and bring to boil. Reduce heat, cover, and simmer until vegetables are tender, about 40 minutes. Add celery stalks and simmer until all vegetables are very tender, about 12 minutes longer. Cool slightly.

Puree soup in blender in batches. Return soup to pot. Add cream. Season with salt and pepper. (*Can be made 1 day ahead. Cover and chill celery leaves. Cool soup slightly. Chill uncovered until cold, then cover and keep chilled. Rewarm soup before serving.*) Ladle into bowls. Garnish with reserved celery leaves.

8 SERVINGS

Cream of Broccoli Soup

    8 cups broccoli florets (about1¼ pounds)

    2 cups low-salt chicken broth
    1 cup plus 4 teaspoons whipping cream
    3 tablespoons unsalted butter
      Ground white pepper

Cook broccoli in large pot of boiling salted water until tender but still bright green, about 5 minutes. Drain broccoli. Set aside 4 small florets for garnish.

Combine broth and 1 cup cream in heavy large saucepan and bring to boil. Working in batches, puree broccoli, broth mixture, and butter in blender until smooth, about 45 seconds per batch. Return puree to same pan. Season soup to taste with salt and white pepper.

Bring soup to simmer, thinning with water if desired. Ladle soup into 4 bowls. Drizzle 1 teaspoon cream over each; garnish with reserved florets.

4 SERVINGS

Zucchini and Spinach Soup

¼ cup olive oil

2 medium onions, chopped

1½ pounds zucchini, trimmed, cut into ½-inch-thick rounds

1 12-ounce russet potato, peeled, thinly sliced

4 cups (or more) low-salt chicken broth

1 6-ounce bag baby spinach leaves

1½ cups coarsely chopped cilantro

Heat oil in large pot over medium heat. Add onions; sauté until soft, about 8 minutes. Add zucchini and potato; stir to coat. Add 4 cups broth and bring soup to boil. Reduce heat to medium-low, cover, and simmer until potato is soft, about 15 minutes. Working in batches, puree soup in blender until smooth, adding some spinach and cilantro to each batch. Return puree to same pot. Thin with more broth by ¼ cupfuls, if desired. Season soup with salt and pepper. *(Can be made 1 day ahead. Chill until cold, then cover and keep refrigerated. Rewarm soup before serving.)*

8 SERVINGS

Chilled Cucumber Soup with Smoked Salmon and Dill

1½ tablespoons butter
1 cup chopped onions
4 cucumbers, peeled, halved, seeded, cut crosswise into ½-inch-thick slices (about 5 cups)
1 8-ounce russet potato, peeled, cut into ½-inch dice
3½ cups low-salt chicken broth
3 large fresh dill sprigs plus 6 tablespoons minced fresh dill
1 teaspoon (or more) salt

1 cup crème fraîche or sour cream
3 ounces smoked salmon, cut into ½-inch pieces

Melt butter in heavy large pot over medium heat. Add onions and sauté until slightly softened, about 3 minutes. Add cucumbers and potato; stir 1 minute. Add broth, dill sprigs, and 1 teaspoon salt. Increase heat and bring to simmer. Reduce heat to low; cover and simmer until cucumbers and potato are tender, stirring occasionally, about 25 minutes.

Working in batches, puree soup in processor. Return to pot. Cool 15 minutes. Whisk in ½ cup crème fraîche and 4 tablespoons minced dill. Cover; chill until cold, about 4 hours. *(Can be made 1 day ahead. Keep chilled.)* Add more salt to taste, if desired. Ladle into 6 bowls. Top with crème fraîche; sprinkle with smoked salmon and 2 tablespoons minced dill.

6 SERVINGS

Leek, Potato, and Tarragon Soup

3 tablespoons butter
2 leeks (white and pale green parts only), sliced (about 2 cups)
1 small onion, chopped
4 garlic cloves, sliced
2 tablespoons water
½ pound red-skinned potatoes, unpeeled, cut into ½-inch pieces
4 cups low-salt chicken broth or vegetable broth
2 teaspoons chopped fresh tarragon
½ cup whipping cream
½ cup plain whole yogurt

Melt butter in heavy large pot over medium heat. Add leeks, onion, garlic, and 2 tablespoons water. Cook until leeks are just golden, about 10 minutes. Add potatoes and broth; bring to boil. Reduce heat to low and simmer until potatoes are tender, about 10 minutes. Mix in tarragon. Stir in cream and yogurt. Season soup to taste with salt and pepper.

4 TO 6 SERVINGS

Banana Piña Coladas

3 12-ounce cans evaporated milk
3 8-ounce cans unsweetened
  pineapple chunks in juice,
  undrained
3 large bananas, sliced
36 ice cubes
1½ cups refrigerated pineapple-
  orange-banana juice blend
1 cup golden rum or 1½ teaspoons
  rum extract
1½ teaspoons coconut extract

Puree ⅓ of all ingredients in blender. Transfer to pitcher. Repeat with remaining ingredients in 2 batches.

10 SERVINGS

Key West Citrus Coolers

6 cups water
3 cups sugar

3 cups fresh lime juice
3 cups orange juice
  Crushed ice

Bring 3 cups water and sugar to boil in large saucepan over high heat, stirring until sugar dissolves. Boil 3 minutes. Transfer syrup to bowl; cover. Chill until cold, at least 3 hours and up to 1 week.

Mix lime juice, orange juice, 3 cups syrup, and 3 cups water in large pitcher. (*Can be made 1 day ahead. Cover; chill.*) Fill glasses with ice. Pour cooler over.

10 SERVINGS

BEVERAGES

Blush Bellinis

1½ cups frozen sliced peaches, thawed
1 cup peach nectar
½ cup sugar
¾ cup frozen orange-peach-mango concentrate, thawed
3 frozen or fresh raspberries
2 750-ml bottles chilled Champagne

Combine peaches, peach nectar, sugar, fruit concentrate, and 3 raspberries in processor; blend until smooth. Strain fruit puree into bowl, stirring to extract as much liquid as possible. (*Can be made 1 day ahead. Cover; chill.*)

Pour ⅓ cup fruit puree into each of 8 Champagne flutes. Fill flutes with Champagne; stir gently.

8 SERVINGS

A few raspberries give these drinks a vibrant color. Blending the peach puree the day before makes last-minute drink prep a snap: Simply add Champagne as people arrive. There's extra peach puree if anybody wants seconds.

Blues Mojito

2 cups sugar
2 cups water

1½ cups fresh lime juice
16 fresh mint leaves
Crushed ice
2 cups white rum
4 teaspoons blue curaçao (optional)
2⅔ cups club soda
Fresh mint sprigs

Stir sugar and 2 cups water in saucepan over medium-low heat until sugar dissolves (do not boil). Transfer syrup to bowl. (*Can be made 1 week ahead. Cover; chill.*)

In each of 8 highball glasses, place 3 tablespoons syrup, 3 tablespoons lime juice, and 2 mint leaves. Stir, crushing mint to release flavor. Fill each glass with crushed ice, then ¼ cup rum and ½ teaspoon curaçao, if desired. Pour in ⅓ cup soda and garnish with mint.

8 SERVINGS

Frozen Limes Filled with Sangrita and Tequila

12 limes, ends trimmed, cut crosswise in half

2¼ cups fresh orange juice

5 tablespoons grenadine syrup

1 teaspoon (generous) salt

1 teaspoon cayenne pepper

Premium tequila

Squeeze lime halves in citrus juicer to extract as much juice as possible. Transfer ³⁄₄ cup lime juice to bowl; cover and chill. Reserve remaining juice for another use. Using scissors, cut out membranes from hollowed lime halves. Enclose lime cups in resealable plastic bag. Freeze until frozen, about 4 hours.

Mix orange juice, ³⁄₄ cup lime juice, grenadine, salt, and cayenne in blender. Transfer mixture to pitcher. Cover sangrita and refrigerate until cold, about 2 hours. *(Sangrita can*

be prepared 1 day ahead. Keep sangrita chilled. Keep lime cups frozen.)

Arrange frozen lime cups on serving tray. Pour sangrita into 12 lime cups; pour tequila into remaining 12 lime cups and serve immediately.

12 SERVINGS

Classic Shaken Margaritas

 1 lime, cut crosswise into 5 slices
   Coarse kosher salt

 1 cup ice cubes
 ½ cup premium tequila
 ¼ cup triple sec or other orange liqueur
 2 tablespoons fresh lime juice

Place 3 lime slices in single layer on small plate. Pour enough salt on another small plate to reach depth of ¼ inch. Lightly press rims of 2 Margarita glasses onto lime slices, twisting to extract juices and coat rims. Dip moistened rims into salt to coat lightly.

Combine ice cubes, tequila, triple sec, and lime juice in cocktail shaker. Shake until outside of shaker becomes frosty. Strain mixture into prepared glasses. Garnish rims with 2 remaining lime slices and serve immediately.

MAKES 2

Mexican and Key limes are sweeter than Persian limes (the standard supermarket variety). They can often be found at Latin American markets or at local farmers' markets. Make these Margaritas two at a time.

Hibiscus Flower Water

 8 cups water
 ½ cup (packed) golden brown sugar
 ¾ cup jamaica (hibiscus) flowers (about 1½ ounces)

   Ice cubes
   Assorted orange, lemon, and lime slices (for garnish)

Bring 8 cups water to boil in large pot. Add sugar and flowers. Return water to boil, stirring to dissolve sugar. Reduce heat and simmer uncovered 10 minutes to blend flavors. Strain liquid into pitcher. Chill until cold. *(Can be made 1 day ahead. Cover and keep chilled.)*

Fill glasses with ice cubes and citrus slices. Pour liquid over and serve immediately.

6 SERVINGS

Mexico has a wonderful variety of sweetened flavored waters known as *aguas frescas*. They are made from citrus fruits, melons, and cucumbers. Among the most popular is this one, made by steeping the dried, deep crimson calyxes of hibiscus flowers which are found in Latin American markets and some specialty stores. This slightly tart, garnet-colored beverage is beautiful and refreshing.

Strawberry-Kiwi Sangria with Rose Geranium

- 8 cups water
- 8 wild-berry tea bags
- 2 cups sugar

- 4 1-pint baskets strawberries, hulled
- 2 25.4-ounce (750-ml) bottles chilled sparkling apple cider
- 6 kiwis, peeled, cut into ½-inch cubes
- 16 fresh rose geranium leaves, crushed slightly, or ¾ teaspoon rose water*
- 4 cups ice cubes

Bring 4 cups water to boil in large saucepan. Add tea bags; cover and let steep 10 minutes. Discard tea bags. Add sugar to hot tea; stir until dissolved. Stir in remaining 4 cups water. Chill tea until cold, about 3 hours. (Can be made 1 day ahead. Cover; keep chilled.)

Puree 2 baskets strawberries in processor. Slice remaining 2 baskets strawberries. Place pureed and sliced berries in large pitcher (or divide between 2 pitchers). Add tea and all remaining ingredients. Stir and serve.

*Rose water is available at Middle Eastern markets and specialty foods stores.

12 SERVINGS

This sweetly refreshing summer cooler contains no alcohol, but the wild-berry tea and pureed strawberries give it that sangria color. For guests who prefer their beverages a bit more spirited, you can add white Muscat or light rum to taste. Unless you already grow them, you'll most likely have to visit a nursery to find rose geraniums. They make great potted plants and, of course, smell wonderful, too. The aromatic, rose-scented leaves are used to infuse their flavor in sorbets, ices, and beverages.

Spiced Apple Cider

- 1 large orange
- 4 quarts apple cider
- ¼ cup (packed) golden brown sugar
- 2 tablespoons fresh lemon juice
- 15 whole cloves
- 10 whole allspice
- 8 whole green cardamom pods, crushed
- 5 cinnamon sticks, each broken in half

Using vegetable peeler, remove peel (orange part only) from orange in strips. Place orange peel in heavy large pot (reserve orange for another use). Add apple cider and all remaining ingredients to pot. Bring to boil, stirring until sugar dissolves. Reduce heat to medium-low; simmer until mixture is reduced to generous 8 cups, about 40 minutes. Strain into medium pot. Rewarm cider. Ladle into mugs.

MAKES ABOUT 8 CUPS

Roasted Beef Tenderloin
Wrapped in Bacon (page 48)

Main Courses

Meats

Poultry

Seafood

Meatless

Pasta & Pizza

Pan-Grilled New York Strip Steaks with Green Olive Tapenade

½ cup slivered almonds, toasted
1 pound mild green brine-cured olives (such as Picholine), pitted
5 tablespoons olive oil
2 tablespoons drained capers
4 anchovy fillets
2 garlic cloves

2 2-inch-thick New York strip steaks (each about 1¼ pounds)
2 tablespoons chopped fresh rosemary

Place almonds in processor and grind finely; transfer to small bowl. Place olives, oil, capers, anchovies, and garlic in processor. Blend until fine paste forms. Add almonds; blend 5 seconds. Season tapenade with salt and pepper. *(Can be made 2 days ahead. Cover; chill.)*

Sprinkle steaks generously with salt and pepper. Coat steaks with rosemary, pressing to adhere. Heat 2 heavy medium skillets (preferably cast-iron) over high heat 5 minutes.

Place 1 steak in each pan. Sear steaks 3 minutes; turn over and sear second side 3 minutes. Reduce heat to medium-high. Continue to cook, turning every 3 minutes, until steaks are cooked to desired doneness, about 15 minutes longer for medium-rare (thermometer inserted into center of steaks will register 130°F). Transfer steaks to platter; let stand 10 minutes. Slice steaks thinly. Serve with tapenade.

6 SERVINGS

MEATS

Napa Valley Cabernet Burgers

1	750-ml bottle Cabernet Sauvignon
¼	cup minced shallots
9	tablespoons unsalted butter, room temperature
2	teaspoons golden brown sugar
1	tablespoon minced fresh rosemary

1½	pounds ground beef (15% fat)
1	teaspoon salt
½	teaspoon ground black pepper
	Vegetable oil
1	cup (packed) coarsely grated extra-sharp white cheddar cheese

4	4½-inch squares focaccia, cut horizontally in half
8	large tomato slices
2	cups arugula

Boil wine and shallots in medium saucepan until reduced to ¾ cup, about 20 minutes. Add 1 tablespoon butter and brown sugar; whisk until butter melts and sugar dissolves. Remove from heat. Mix 8 tablespoons butter and rosemary in small bowl. Set aside.

Prepare barbecue (medium-high heat). Mix beef, salt, pepper, and ¼ cup wine-shallot mixture in bowl. Form meat into four 5-inch squares or rounds. Brush grill rack with oil. Grill burgers until brown on bottom, about 3 minutes. Turn burgers and brush with wine-shallot mixture. Continue grilling burgers until cooked to desired doneness, turning and brushing occasionally with wine-shallot mixture, about 4 minutes longer for medium-rare. Sprinkle with cheese after last turn and grill until cheese melts.

Spread cut sides of bread with rosemary butter. Grill, cut side down, until golden, about 2 minutes. Arrange bread, grilled side up, on plates. Top bottom halves with burgers, then tomatoes and arugula. Cover with top halves of bread.

4 SERVINGS

Meatballs in Mexican Tomato Sauce

MEATBALLS

  4 4x4-inch crustless squares firm white sandwich bread, torn into small pieces

 ⅓ cup whole milk

 ¼ cup finely chopped white onion

  3 garlic cloves, minced

  2 teaspoons fine sea salt

  1 teaspoon dried oregano

 ½ teaspoon ground black pepper

  1 pound lean ground beef

  1 pound lean ground pork

  1 cup finely chopped seeded tomatoes (about 4 medium)

  2 large eggs

 ¼ cup chopped fresh mint

SAUCE

  4 medium serrano chiles, stemmed

  2 garlic cloves, unpeeled

  4 14½-ounce cans diced tomatoes in juice

 ¼ cup canola oil

  1 cup water

  1 teaspoon fine sea salt

     Cooked white rice

FOR MEATBALLS: Combine first 7 ingredients in large bowl. Mash with fork until thick paste forms. Mix in beef, pork, tomatoes, eggs, and mint (mixture will be soft). Using ¼ cupful for each, form mixture into 2-inch balls. Place on baking sheet; chill while making sauce.

FOR SAUCE: Line heavy small skillet with foil; add chiles and garlic. Cook over medium-high heat until skins begin to blister and blacken, turning frequently, about 15 minutes. Cool garlic slightly, then peel. Working in batches, puree tomatoes with juices, whole chiles, and garlic in blender until almost smooth. *(Meatballs and puree can be prepared 6 hours ahead. Keep meatballs refrigerated. Cover and refrigerate puree.)*

Heat oil in heavy large wide pot over medium-high heat. Add tomato puree, 1 cup water, and salt; bring to boil. Carefully add meatballs; bring to simmer. Reduce heat, cover, and simmer until cooked through, stirring occasionally, about 30 minutes. Uncover; boil gently until liquid is reduced to sauce consistency, stirring occasionally, about 18 minutes.

Spoon rice into 6 shallow bowls. Top with meatballs and sauce.

6 SERVINGS

Flemish Beef Stew

- 6 bacon slices, coarsely chopped
- 2¼ pounds beef tenderloin, trimmed, cut into 1½-inch pieces
- ⅓ cup all purpose flour

- 1 very large onion, sliced
- 3 large garlic cloves, minced
- 4 cups canned beef broth
- 1 cup beer
- ¼ cup tomato paste
- 3 tablespoons chopped fresh thyme
- 2 tablespoons dark brown sugar
- 4 tablespoons chopped fresh parsley

Cook bacon in heavy large pot over medium heat until crisp, about 5 minutes. Using slotted spoon, transfer bacon to paper towels to drain. Reserve bacon drippings in pot.

Sprinkle beef with salt and pepper. Place flour in large bowl. Toss meat in flour, shaking off excess and reserving remaining flour in bowl. Heat drippings in pot over medium-high heat. Working in 2 batches, add beef to pot and cook until just browned, stirring frequently, about 5 minutes per batch. Transfer meat to large bowl.

Add onion and garlic to pot and sauté until tender, about 5 minutes. Add remaining flour and stir 1 minute. Mix in broth, beer, tomato paste, 2 tablespoons thyme, and sugar. Reduce heat to medium; simmer until mixture thickens slightly, scraping up browned bits, about 15 minutes. Add beef, 1 tablespoon thyme, and 3 tablespoons parsley. Simmer until beef is cooked as desired, about 5 minutes for medium-rare. Season with salt and pepper. Transfer stew to bowls, sprinkle with 1 tablespoon parsley and reserved bacon bits, and serve.

4 SERVINGS

South-of-the-Border Dinner for 6

Brie and Walnut Quesadillas with Tropical Fruit Salsa
(page 16)

Classic Shaken Margaritas
(page 39; triple recipe)

Meatballs in Mexican Tomato Sauce
(opposite)

Romaine Salad with Chipotle Dressing and Warm Queso Fresco
(page 151)

Zinfandel

Dulce de Leche Ice Cream

Coffee with Cinnamon

Roasted Beef Tenderloin Wrapped in Bacon

- 1 3-pound beef tenderloin piece (large end), trimmed
- 12 ¼-inch-thick slices peeled garlic (from about 4 cloves)
- 1 tablespoon coarsely ground black pepper
- 1 pound bacon slices
- 3 8- to 9-inch-long fresh rosemary branches

Preheat oven to 450°F. Using small sharp knife, cut twelve 1-inch-deep slits all over beef tenderloin. Insert garlic slices into slits. Rub pepper all over tenderloin. Arrange bacon slices on work surface, overlapping slightly and forming rectangle. Place 1 rosemary branch down center of bacon rectangle, perpendicular to bacon slices. Place tenderloin atop rosemary branch. Place remaining 2 rosemary branches atop tenderloin. Wrap bacon slices around tenderloin and rosemary to enclose tenderloin completely. Place tenderloin in roasting pan, bacon ends down. *(Can be assembled 1 day ahead. Cover and refrigerate.)*

Roast tenderloin until meat thermometer inserted into center registers 125°F for rare, about 1 hour. Remove from oven. Tent with foil and let tenderloin stand 10 minutes.

Transfer tenderloin to cutting board. Using large sharp knife, cut tenderloin through bacon and rosemary into ¹/₂-inch-thick slices and serve.

8 SERVINGS

Barbecued Cowboy Steaks

- 1 tablespoon coarse kosher salt
- 1 teaspoon Hungarian sweet paprika
- 1 teaspoon garlic powder
- 1 teaspoon coarsely ground black pepper
- 1 teaspoon dried ground thyme
- 1 teaspoon finely ground coffee beans
- 4 1¼- to 1½-inch-thick bone-in beef rib steaks (each weighing 12 to 16 ounces)

- 1 2.2-pound bag instant-light mesquite chunks
- 1 cup mesquite or hickory wood smoke chips, soaked in cold water at least 30 minutes

Mix first 6 ingredients in small bowl. Sprinkle spice rub over both sides of steaks, pressing to adhere. Let steaks stand at room temperature 1 hour.

Spread entire bag of instant-light mesquite chunks over ²/₃ of bottom rack and prepare barbecue (medium-high heat). Grill steaks over mesquite until brown on both sides, about 2 minutes per side. Remove steaks from grill. Let mesquite chunks burn until ash is gray.

Drain wood chips; scatter over mesquite. Return steaks to cooler part of grill (not over mesquite). Cover barbecue with lid; grill steaks to desired doneness, about 10 minutes for medium-rare. Let steaks rest 5 minutes before serving.

4 TO 8 SERVINGS

Grilled Flank Steak with Chimichurri Sauce

  1 cup extra-virgin olive oil
  ½ cup (about 15) peeled garlic cloves
  ⅓ cup Sherry wine vinegar
  ¼ cup chopped fresh parsley
  ¼ cup chopped fresh cilantro
  ¼ cup fresh oregano leaves
  3 tablespoons fresh thyme leaves

  ¼ cup (½ stick) butter

  2 1½-pound flat iron steaks
  3 cups oak- or hickory-wood smoke chips, soaked in cold water at least 30 minutes, drained
  1 8-inch square disposable aluminum foil baking pan

Finely chop first 7 ingredients in processor. Set sauce aside.

Cook butter in small heavy saucepan over medium-high heat until brown, about 2 minutes. Add sauce; stir 1 minute. Season sauce with salt and pepper.

Prepare barbecue (medium-high heat). Sprinkle steaks with salt and pepper. Place soaked wood chips in foil pan. Place pan directly atop coals on barbecue. When chips begin to smoke, place steaks on grill rack directly over chips and cook to desired doneness, about 4 minutes per side for medium-rare. Remove steaks from grill; let stand 5 minutes. Thinly slice steaks across grain. Serve with sauce.

6 TO 8 SERVINGS

Chimichurri sauce, a fresh herb and garlic sauce, is a popular accompaniment to beef in Argentina.

Filet Mignon with Rajas

- 3 fresh poblano chiles
- 1 tablespoon vegetable oil
- 1 tablespoon olive oil
- ½ small white onion, thinly sliced
- ½ cup whipping cream
- 4 6-ounce filet mignons (each about 1½ to 2 inches thick)

Char chiles over gas flame or in broiler until blackened on all sides. Enclose in paper bag. Let stand 10 minutes. Peel and seed chiles; slice thinly. Heat both oils in large skillet over medium heat. Add onion and sauté until translucent, about 2 minutes. Add poblanos and cream; simmer until rajas thicken slightly, about 3 minutes. Season with salt.

Meanwhile, prepare barbecue (medium-high heat). Sprinkle steaks with salt. Grill steaks to desired doneness, about 5 minutes per side for medium-rare. Transfer to plates; top with rajas and serve.

4 SERVINGS

The mild flavor of the meat is revved up with rich *rajas con crema*, a traditional Mexican dish of roasted poblano strips in cream.

Beef Short Ribs in Chipotle and Green Chile Sauce

      1 teaspoon salt
      1 teaspoon freshly ground black pepper
      1 teaspoon ground cumin
      1 teaspoon chili powder
    ½ teaspoon ground coriander
      8 3-inch-long meaty beef short ribs

      2 tablespoons olive oil
   1½ cups chopped onion
      6 large garlic cloves, minced
      1 14-ounce can low-salt chicken broth
      1 cup drained canned diced tomatoes
    ¼ cup fresh lime juice
   1½ tablespoons chopped canned chipotle chiles*

      3 large fresh Anaheim (California) chiles, stemmed, seeded, cut into ¼-inch-thick rings
         Chopped fresh cilantro
         Lime wedges

Mix first 5 ingredients in bowl; sprinkle all over short ribs. Place ribs on plate; cover and chill 1 hour or up to 1 day.

Preheat oven to 350°F. Heat oil in large ovenproof pot over medium-high heat. Add half of ribs and brown on all sides, about 9 minutes; transfer to plate. Repeat with remaining ribs. Reduce heat to medium. Add chopped onion and garlic to same pot; cover and cook until onion is soft, stirring occasionally, about 5 minutes. Add chicken broth and bring to boil, scraping up browned bits. Add tomatoes, fresh lime juice, and chipotle chiles. Return ribs to pot, meaty side down, in single layer. Bring to boil; cover and cook in oven until ribs are just tender, about 1½ hours.

Remove pot from oven. Tilt pot; spoon off fat. Place pot over medium heat and simmer uncovered until sauce coats spoon and ribs are very tender, about 25 minutes. Season sauce with salt and pepper. (*Can be made 1 day ahead. Cool 30 minutes, refrigerate uncovered until cold, then cover and keep refrigerated.*)

Bring ribs to simmer over medium heat; add chile rings. Simmer until chiles soften, about 10 minutes. Transfer ribs and sauce to bowls. Top with cilantro; garnish with lime.

Chipotle chiles canned in a spicy tomato sauce, sometimes called adobo, *are available at Latin American markets, specialty foods stores, and some supermarkets.*

4 SERVINGS

Lemon-Parsley Veal Chops

VEAL

- ½ cup olive oil
- 6 tablespoons fresh lemon juice
- ⅓ cup chopped fresh Italian parsley
- 3 garlic cloves, crushed
- 1 tablespoon minced fresh rosemary
- 6 8- to 10-ounce loin or rib veal chops, each about 1 inch thick

TOPPING

- 3 tablespoons chopped fresh Italian parsley
- 1 tablespoon grated lemon peel
- 1½ teaspoons minced fresh rosemary
- 1 teaspoon minced garlic

FOR VEAL: Whisk first 5 ingredients in small bowl to blend. Arrange veal chops in 15x10x2-inch glass baking dish. Sprinkle chops on both sides with salt and pepper. Pour marinade over chops; turn to coat. Cover and refrigerate at least 6 hours or overnight, turning occasionally.

FOR TOPPING: Stir together parsley, lemon peel, rosemary, and garlic in small bowl to blend.

Prepare barbecue (medium-high heat). Remove chops from marinade and sprinkle generously with salt and pepper. Grill chops until cooked to desired doneness, about 6 minutes per side for medium-rare. Transfer chops to serving platter; sprinkle each with topping.

6 SERVINGS

Veal Cutlets with Sautéed Baby Artichokes

¼ cup fresh lemon juice
12 baby artichokes

¼ cup olive oil
2 large garlic cloves, minced
6 large ripe plum tomatoes, each cut into 6 wedges
½ teaspoon dried crushed red pepper
½ cup fresh basil leaves, thinly sliced
1 teaspoon grated lemon peel

6 4-ounce veal cutlets (each about ¼ to ⅓ inch thick)
2 tablespoons (¼ stick) butter
3 tablespoons chopped fresh parsley

Fill large bowl with cold water; add lemon juice. Cut off stem and top quarter from 1 artichoke. Bend back dark green outer leaves and snap off at base until pale green and yellow leaves remain. Quarter artichoke lengthwise; remove any purple-tipped leaves from center. Place in lemon water. Repeat with remaining artichokes.

Cook drained artichokes in large pot of boiling salted water until crisp-tender, about 8 minutes. Drain well; set aside.

Heat oil in heavy large skillet over medium-high heat. Add garlic and sauté until fragrant, about 1 minute. Add artichokes and sauté 5 minutes. Add tomatoes and crushed red pepper. Cook until tomatoes soften, about 5 minutes. Stir in basil and lemon peel. Season to taste with salt and pepper. (*Can be made 2 hours ahead. Cover and let stand at room temperature. Rewarm before using.*)

Sprinkle veal with salt and pepper. Melt butter in large nonstick skillet over high heat. Working in batches, add veal and cook until brown, about 2 minutes per side. Transfer veal to plates. Sprinkle with parsley. Serve with artichoke mixture.

6 SERVINGS

Farmers' Market Dinner for 6

Shrimp Risotto with Spinach and Basil
(*page 12*)

Veal Cutlets with Sautéed Baby Artichokes
(*at left*)

Mixed Green Salad

Pinot Gris

Apple Crostata with Crystallized Ginger
(*page 172*)

Lamb Shanks with Fresh Herbs

2 teaspoons salt
2 teaspoons chopped fresh rosemary
2 teaspoons chopped fresh thyme
1 teaspoon fennel seeds
1 teaspoon freshly ground black pepper
½ teaspoon ground coriander
4 large lamb shanks

3 tablespoons olive oil
2 ounces thinly sliced capocollo or pancetta, cut into thin strips
1½ cups chopped onion
1 cup chopped carrots
½ cup chopped celery
6 garlic cloves, chopped
3 3x½-inch strips lemon peel
2 small bay leaves
2 teaspoons chopped fresh thyme
2 cups dry white wine
2 cups drained canned diced tomatoes in juice
1½ cups low-salt chicken broth

3 tablespoons chopped fresh parsley
1 tablespoon grated lemon peel
½ teaspoon freshly ground black pepper

Mix first 6 ingredients in small bowl; rub all over lamb. Let stand 30 minutes.

Preheat oven to 350°F. Heat oil in large ovenproof pot over medium-high heat. Add lamb and sauté until brown, turning with tongs, about 12 minutes; transfer to plate. Reduce heat to medium. Add capocollo and stir 1 minute. Add onion, carrots, and celery. Cover and cook until vegetables are soft, stirring occasionally, about 10 minutes. Mix in garlic; cook 1 minute. Mix in lemon peel strips, bay leaves, and thyme. Add wine and bring to boil, scraping up browned bits. Add tomatoes and broth. Return lamb to pot. Bring to boil; cover and transfer pot to oven.

Cook lamb until just tender, turning occasionally, about 1½ hours. Remove pot from oven. Tilt pot and spoon off fat that rises to top of sauce. Place pot over medium heat and boil uncovered until sauce reduces enough to coat spoon and lamb is very tender, about 30 minutes. Season to taste with salt and pepper. Discard lemon peel and bay leaves. (*Can be made 1 day ahead. Cool 30 minutes, chill uncovered until cold, then cover and keep chilled. Rewarm over low heat before continuing.*)

Mix parsley, grated lemon peel, and ½ teaspoon pepper in small bowl for gremolata. Transfer lamb to large shallow bowl. Sprinkle with gremolata and serve.

4 SERVINGS

Barbecued Rack of Lamb with Tomato-Mint Dressing

16 whole cloves
 2 well-trimmed 8-rib racks of lamb, each about 1¼ pounds, each cut into 4 double chops
⅔ cup olive oil
½ cup chopped fresh mint
¼ cup white wine vinegar
 1 tablespoon whole grain Dijon mustard

 2 plum tomatoes, seeded, chopped

Press 2 whole cloves, close to bone, into each double lamb chop. Arrange chops in 13x9x2-inch glass baking dish. Whisk oil, mint, vinegar, and mustard in small bowl to blend. Season dressing generously with salt and pepper. Spoon ⅓ cup dressing over lamb and turn to coat evenly; reserve remaining dressing in bowl. Let lamb marinate at room temperature 2 hours or cover and refrigerate up to 6 hours, turning lamb occasionally.

Prepare barbecue (medium-high heat). Mix tomatoes into reserved dressing in bowl. Grill lamb until cooked to desired doneness, turning occasionally, about 10 minutes for medium-rare. Transfer lamb chops to platter; spoon tomato-mint dressing over and serve.

4 SERVINGS

Roast Leg of Lamb with Fennel Butter

SEASONED BUTTER

- 6 tablespoons (¾ stick) butter, room temperature
- 3 tablespoons fennel seeds, crushed in plastic bag with mallet
- 3 large garlic cloves, minced
- 2 tablespoons Dijon mustard
- 1½ tablespoons soy sauce
- 1 tablespoon coarsely ground black pepper
- 1½ teaspoons dried crushed rosemary

LAMB

- 2 tablespoons olive oil
- 1 6- to 6½-pound bone-in leg of lamb, well trimmed
- 2 cups dry red wine
- 1⅓ cups low-salt chicken broth
- Fresh rosemary sprigs (optional)

FOR SEASONED BUTTER: Mix all ingredients with fork in medium bowl. (*Can be made 1 day ahead. Cover and refrigerate. Bring to room temperature before using.*)

FOR LAMB: Position rack in bottom third of oven and preheat to 450°F. Pour 2 tablespoons oil into large roasting pan. Place pan directly atop 2 burners over medium-high heat. Sprinkle lamb with salt and pepper. Add lamb to pan and brown on all sides, about 8 minutes total. Remove pan from heat. Brush lamb with half of seasoned butter.

Roast lamb 30 minutes. Reduce heat to 350°F; continue roasting until thermometer inserted into thickest part of meat registers 130°F for medium-rare, about 40 minutes longer. Transfer to platter; tent with foil. Let stand 20 minutes.

Skim off fat from drippings in roasting pan. Place pan atop 2 burners over high heat. Add wine and broth. Boil until mixture is reduced to 2 cups, about 13 minutes. Whisk in remaining seasoned butter (sauce will be thin). Season sauce to taste with salt and pepper.

Garnish lamb with rosemary sprigs, if desired. Serve with sauce.

6 TO 8 SERVINGS

Birthday Dinner for 6

Curried Wild Mushroom Pâté
(page 10)

Roast Leg of Lamb with
Fennel Butter
(at left)

Potatoes Roasted with Olive Oil
and Bay Leaves
(page 144)

Sautéed Spinach

Bordeaux

Triple-Layer White Cake with
Orange Curd Filling
and Frosting
(page 206)

Moroccan Lamb Kebabs with Golden Couscous

¾ cup olive oil

⅔ cup fresh lemon juice

6 large garlic cloves, minced

2 tablespoons chopped fresh mint

4 teaspoons salt

4 teaspoons grated lemon peel

2 teaspoons ground black pepper

2 teaspoons ground coriander

1 teaspoon ground cumin

4 pounds well-trimmed boneless leg of lamb, cut into 2-inch cubes

16 12-inch-long metal skewers

32 whole dried apricots (preferably Mediterranean), soaked in boiling water 5 minutes, drained

4 red onions, each cut into 8 chunks

Golden Couscous (see recipe opposite)

Whisk first 9 ingredients in medium bowl to blend. Transfer ½ cup marinade to small bowl; cover, chill, and reserve as basting sauce. Add lamb to remaining marinade in medium bowl; toss to coat. Marinate 2 hours at room temperature or cover and refrigerate overnight.

Prepare barbecue (medium-high heat). Remove lamb from marinade. Thread lamb cubes onto 8 skewers, dividing equally. Thread apricots and onion chunks alternately on remaining 8 skewers. Brush all skewers with some of reserved ½ cup marinade. Sprinkle onion-apricot skewers with salt and pepper. Grill onion-apricot skewers until onions soften and begin to brown, occasionally turning and basting with marinade and moving skewers to cooler part of barbecue if necessary to keep apricots from burning, about 10 minutes. Grill lamb to desired doneness, turning occasionally, about 8 minutes for medium-rare.

Mound Golden Couscous on platter. Top with skewers and serve.

8 SERVINGS

Golden Couscous

- 6 cups low-salt chicken broth
- 6 tablespoons (¾ stick) butter
- 3 cups chopped onions
- 2 teaspoons ground turmeric
- 1 teaspoon ground cumin
- 3 cups couscous (about 1 pound)
- ⅔ cup slivered almonds, toasted

Bring broth to boil in medium saucepan. Reduce heat to very low; cover to keep hot. Melt butter in heavy large saucepan over medium heat. Add onions; sauté until tender and light golden, about 8 minutes. Add turmeric and cumin; stir 1 minute. Add couscous; stir until coated with onion mixture. Mix in hot broth. Remove from heat. Cover and let stand until broth is absorbed, about 12 minutes. Fluff couscous with fork. Season generously with salt and pepper. Mound on platter. Sprinkle with almonds.

8 SERVINGS

Dinner on the Patio for 8

Toasted Garbanzo Beans and Pistachios with Cumin and Cayenne
(page 19)

Moroccan Lamb Kebabs with Golden Couscous
(opposite)

Garden Salad with Pears and Pine Nuts
(page 152)

Zinfandel

Caramelized Pineapple Sundaes with Chocolate-Coconut Sauce
(page 220)

Lamb Chops with Spicy Peanut Sauce

¾ cup purchased Asian peanut sauce
2 tablespoons soy sauce
1 tablespoon fresh lime juice
1 tablespoon grated fresh ginger
8 ¾- to 1-inch-thick loin lamb chops

Prepare barbecue (medium-high heat). Whisk together first 4 ingredients in small saucepan. Brush 5 tablespoons of sauce over both sides of chops. Reserve remaining sauce.

Grill chops to desired doneness, about 4 minutes per side for medium-rare. Place 2 chops on each of 4 plates. Bring remaining sauce to simmer. Drizzle over lamb and serve.

4 SERVINGS

Basil-Crusted Rack of Lamb

1 large garlic clove
½ cup chopped fresh basil
⅓ cup freshly grated pecorino Romano cheese
⅓ cup plain dry breadcrumbs
2 tablespoons herbes de Provence*
1½ tablespoons Dijon mustard
2½ tablespoons olive oil

1 1½-pound rack of lamb, trimmed

Mince garlic in processor. Add next 5 ingredients. Using on/off turns, process just until basil is finely chopped. Drizzle oil over. Process until mixture is blended. (*Can be made 4 hours ahead. Cover; chill.*)

Preheat oven to 425°F. Sprinkle lamb with salt and pepper. Arrange, bone side down, on small rimmed baking sheet. Press breadcrumb mixture onto lamb, coating completely. Roast until meat thermometer inserted into center of lamb registers 135°F for medium-rare, about 30 minutes. Let lamb rest 15 minutes.

Transfer lamb to cutting board. Cut between bones into individual or double chops. Divide between 2 plates; serve.

A dried herb mixture sold at specialty foods stores and some supermarkets.

2 SERVINGS

Grilled Ham, Cheese, and Salami Sandwiches with Caper Relish

½ cup olive oil

3 tablespoons white wine vinegar

1 large shallot, minced

4 teaspoons minced fresh oregano

1 rectangular 10x7x1½-inch bread loaf (such as ciabatta)

3 ounces sliced provolone cheese

4 ounces sliced Italian Genoa salami

4 ounces sliced Black Forest ham

3 tablespoons finely chopped pitted brine-cured green olives

3 tablespoons capers, chopped

3 tablespoons minced peperoncini

3 tablespoons butter, room temperature

3 ounces Teleme or Fontina cheese, grated (about 1 cup)

1 cup thinly sliced iceberg lettuce

This is an Italian take on the Cuban sandwich called *media noche* ("middle of the night").

Whisk first 4 ingredients in small bowl; season with salt and pepper.

Cut top crust (about ⅓ inch) off bread and discard. Cut bread horizontally in half. Arrange provolone cheese on cut side of bottom half, covering completely. Top with layer of salami, then ham. Mix olives, capers, and peperoncini in small bowl; spread relish over ham. Press top half of bread, cut side down, atop relish; spread with 1½ tablespoons butter.

Heat heavy large skillet over medium heat 3 minutes. Place sandwich, buttered side down, in skillet. Using another skillet, press sandwich to compact slightly. Cook until golden, about 5 minutes. Spread top of sandwich with remaining 1½ tablespoons butter. Using large spatula, turn sandwich over. Press again with second skillet. Cook until bottom is golden and cheese melts, about 5 minutes.

Transfer sandwich to work surface. Lift off bread top; sprinkle with Teleme cheese, lettuce, and dressing. Press bread top onto sandwich and cut into quarters.

4 SERVINGS

Prosciutto-Stuffed Pork Tenderloin with Mushroom Sauce

2	1-pound pork tenderloins
8	thin slices prosciutto (each about 8x2 inches)
½	cup fresh breadcrumbs made from crustless French bread
2	teaspoons chopped fresh rosemary
2	teaspoons chopped fresh thyme
2	tablespoons olive oil
1	teaspoon salt
1	teaspoon freshly ground black pepper
¾	pound mushrooms, sliced
1	garlic clove, minced
1	cup dry white wine
1	cup low-salt chicken broth

This robustly flavorful and sophisticated entrée is the ultimate dinner-party dish. It's also simple to prepare. When shopping, don't buy pork tenderloins that have been pumped with salts and preservatives. Avoid anything that contains ten percent water solution or phosphates.

Arrange tenderloins side by side on work surface with thick end of one next to thin end of other. Slightly overlap prosciutto strips crosswise down length of pork (prosciutto will hang over pork on both sides). Mix breadcrumbs, 1 teaspoon rosemary, and 1 teaspoon thyme in small bowl. Add 1 tablespoon oil; toss to blend. Sprinkle crumb mixture atop prosciutto on 1 pork tenderloin. Fold prosciutto over to cover stuffing and roll second tenderloin over prosciutto and stuffing on first. Using kitchen string, tie tenderloins and stuffing together in 4 or 5 places to make cylinder-shaped roast. Mix salt, pepper, 1 teaspoon rosemary, and 1 teaspoon thyme in small bowl. Rub herb mixture over outside of roast. Let stand 30 minutes.

Preheat oven to 350°F. Heat remaining 1 tablespoon oil in heavy large ovenproof skillet over medium-high heat. Add roast and sauté until brown, turning with tongs, about 7 minutes. Place skillet with roast in oven. Roast pork until thermometer inserted into thickest part of pork registers 145°F, about 35 minutes. Transfer roast to platter; tent loosely with foil to keep warm (temperature will rise 5 to 10 degrees as pork stands).

Place same skillet over medium heat. Add mushrooms and garlic; sauté until mushrooms begin to brown, about 6 minutes. Add wine and broth. Boil until sauce thickens enough to coat spoon, scraping up browned bits, about 12 minutes. Season with salt and pepper.

Cut roast into ½-inch-thick slices; serve with mushroom sauce.

6 SERVINGS

Pork Stew with Fennel and Butternut Squash

3 pounds 2-inch pieces trimmed pork
  shoulder (Boston butt)
2 teaspoons salt
1 teaspoon ground black pepper
1 teaspoon dried rubbed sage
½ teaspoon cayenne pepper
¼ teaspoon ground nutmeg
¼ teaspoon ground ginger

2 tablespoons olive oil
1 cup chopped thinly sliced pancetta* (about
  4 ounces)
2 cups chopped onions
3 garlic cloves, chopped
1 28-ounce can diced tomatoes in juice
2 cups low-salt chicken broth
1 cup dry red wine

2 large fresh fennel bulbs; fronds chopped and reserved, bulbs cut into 1-inch cubes
  (about 5 cups)
20 1½-inch cubes peeled butternut squash (part of 3-pound squash)

Place pork in large bowl. Mix next 6 ingredients in small bowl; sprinkle over pork, turning pork to coat evenly. Let stand 30 minutes.

Preheat oven to 350°F. Heat oil in large ovenproof pot over medium-high heat. Add pancetta and sauté until beginning to brown, about 3 minutes. Using slotted spoon, transfer pancetta to medium bowl. Add half of pork to pot; sauté until brown, about 8 minutes. Using slotted spoon, transfer pork to bowl with pancetta. Repeat with remaining pork. Add onions and garlic to pot; sauté until soft, about 5 minutes. Add tomatoes with juices, broth, wine, and pork mixture. Bring to boil, scraping up browned bits.

Cover pot; place in oven. Cook stew 1 hour. Add fennel bulbs, chopped fronds, and squash cubes to stew. Cover and cook in oven until pork and vegetables are tender, about 30 minutes longer. Using slotted spoon, transfer meat and vegetables to large bowl; cover. Boil sauce over medium-high heat until thickened enough to coat spoon, about 25 minutes. Return meat and vegetables to sauce; season with salt and pepper. (*Can be prepared 1 day ahead. Cool 30 minutes. Refrigerate uncovered until cold, then cover and keep refrigerated.*) Rewarm over low heat.

Pancetta, Italian bacon cured in salt, is available at Italian markets and in the refrigerated deli case of many supermarkets.

6 SERVINGS

Pork Stir-Fry with Green Beans and Peanuts

Supper in the Kitchen for 6

Roasted Red Pepper, Almond, and Garlic Dip
(page 12)

Crudités

Pork Stew with Fennel and Butternut Squash
(opposite; pictured opposite)

Noodles

Mixed Green Salad

Syrah

Pear Clafouti
(page 211)

Coffee

12	ounces pork tenderloin, trimmed, cut into 1½x¼-inch strips
4	tablespoons soy sauce
1½	tablespoons honey
2	garlic cloves, minced
¼	teaspoon dried crushed red pepper
1	pound green beans, trimmed, cut into 1½-inch lengths
1	cup matchstick-size strips peeled carrots (about 2 medium)
2	tablespoons canola oil
1	large red bell pepper, cut into 1½x¼-inch strips
1	tablespoon minced peeled fresh ginger
3	green onions, thinly sliced
¼	cup finely chopped lightly salted dry-roasted peanuts

Mix pork, 1 tablespoon soy sauce, 1 tablespoon honey, half of garlic, and crushed red pepper in medium bowl. Mix 3 tablespoons soy sauce and ½ tablespoon honey in small bowl; set aside.

Cook green beans in large saucepan of boiling salted water until crisp-tender, about 3 minutes. Add carrots to green beans in water; cook 1 minute. Drain carrots and beans.

Heat 1 tablespoon canola oil in wok or large nonstick skillet over high heat. Add pork mixture; stir-fry 1 minute. Transfer pork to dish. Add remaining 1 tablespoon canola oil to wok; add red bell pepper and stir-fry 1 minute. Add green beans, carrots, ginger, and remaining garlic; stir-fry 1 minute. Return pork to wok along with reserved soy sauce-honey mixture; stir until heated through, about 1 minute. Season to taste with salt and pepper. Transfer to bowl. Sprinkle with sliced green onions and chopped peanuts and serve.

4 SERVINGS

Baked Ham with Mustard-Red Currant Glaze and Rhubarb Chutney

¾ cup red currant jelly
6 tablespoons whole grain Dijon mustard
1½ teaspoons ground ginger

1 9-pound fully cooked bone-in ham (shank or butt end)
1 bunch watercress
   Rhubarb Chutney (see recipe below)

Position rack in bottom third of oven and preheat to 325°F. Whisk jelly, mustard, and ginger in heavy medium saucepan over medium heat until melted, about 1 minute. Remove glaze from heat.

Trim any tough rind and fat from upper side of ham, leaving ¼-inch-thick layer of fat. Using long sharp knife, score fat in 1-inch-wide diamond pattern. Place ham in roasting pan. Bake 1 hour. Brush top and sides of ham generously with some of glaze. Bake until thermometer inserted into thickest part of ham registers 140°F, brushing with glaze every 15 minutes and tenting ham with foil if browning too quickly, about 1 hour 15 minutes. Remove ham from oven; let stand 15 minutes. Transfer to platter. Garnish with watercress. Serve with Rhubarb Chutney.

8 SERVINGS

Rhubarb Chutney

1 cup plus 2 tablespoons sugar
½ cup red wine vinegar
1½ cinnamon sticks
1½ tablespoons minced fresh ginger
1½ teaspoons grated orange peel
½ teaspoon (scant) ground cardamom
4½ cups coarsely chopped rhubarb (from 1¾ pounds rhubarb)
¾ cup dried currants
4 green onions, chopped

Stir first 6 ingredients in heavy large saucepan over medium heat until sugar dissolves and mixture boils. Add rhubarb, currants, and green onions; bring to boil. Reduce heat and simmer until rhubarb is tender but not falling apart, about 4 minutes. Cool to room temperature. Discard cinnamon. Cover and chill chutney until cold, at least 1 hour. *(Can be made up to 2 days ahead. Keep chilled.)* Bring to room temperature before serving.

MAKES ABOUT 4 CUPS

Smothered Grilled Pork Chops

  2 large red bell peppers
  2 tablespoons plus 4 teaspoons vegetable oil
  2 medium onions, thinly sliced
  1 tablespoon all purpose flour
¼ cup dry white wine
  2 tablespoons apple cider vinegar
  2 tablespoons drained capers
  1 cup low-salt chicken broth
  1 tablespoon chopped fresh parsley

  4 1- to 1¼-inch-thick bone-in rib pork chops (each about 12 ounces)

Char peppers over gas flame, in broiler, or on grill until charred on all sides. Enclose in paper bag 10 minutes. Peel and seed peppers; slice into thin strips. Heat 2 tablespoons oil in large skillet over medium heat. Add onions and sauté until golden, about 15 minutes. Mix in flour; sauté 2 minutes. Add bell peppers, wine, vinegar, and capers; cook 1 minute. Add broth. Increase heat; boil until sauce thickens enough to coat spoon, about 4 minutes. Mix in parsley. Season with salt and pepper. *(Can be prepared 1 day ahead. Cover and refrigerate. Rewarm before using.)*

Prepare barbecue (medium-high heat). Brush pork on all sides with remaining 4 teaspoons oil. Sprinkle pork with salt and pepper. Grill until thermometer inserted into center of pork registers 145°F, about 10 minutes per side. Transfer chops to platter. Spoon sauce over.

4 SERVINGS

Summer Evening Supper for 8

Creamy White Bean Dip
(page 10)

Smothered Grilled Pork Chops
(at left; pictured on cover; double recipe)

Grilled Corn Salad with Lima Beans and Tomatoes
(page 160; pictured on the cover)

Sauvignon Blanc

Sorbet and Ice Cream Terrine with Blackberry Compote
(page 222)

Baby Back Ribs with Hot and Smoky Barbecue Sauce

- 1 tablespoon garlic powder
- 1 tablespoon chili powder
- 2 teaspoons ground cumin
- 2 teaspoons salt
- 1 teaspoon coarsely ground black pepper
- ½ teaspoon ground allspice
- 6 to 7 pounds meaty baby back pork ribs, cut into 6- to 7-rib slabs

Hot and Smoky Barbecue Sauce (see recipe below)

Combine garlic powder, chili powder, cumin, salt, coarsely ground black pepper, and allspice in small bowl; whisk to blend. Sprinkle 1 teaspoon spice rub on each side of each slab of ribs. Arrange on large baking sheet; cover with foil and chill at least 2 hours and up to 1 day.

Prepare barbecue (medium heat). Arrange ribs on rack and grill until tender and cooked through, turning occasionally, about 35 minutes.

Reserve 2 cups barbecue sauce in small bowl. Brush each side of each pork rib slab generously with some of remaining barbecue sauce. Continue grilling until ribs are heated through and sauce forms sticky coating, about 4 minutes per side. Transfer ribs to platter. Cut slabs between bones into individual ribs and serve, passing reserved 2 cups barbecue sauce alongside.

8 SERVINGS

Hot and Smoky Barbecue Sauce

- 4 8-ounce cans tomato sauce
- 2 cups chopped red onions
- ¾ cup apple cider vinegar
- 6 tablespoons (packed) dark brown sugar
- ¼ cup chili powder
- 8 large garlic cloves, minced
- 2 tablespoons olive oil
- 1 tablespoon liquid smoke*
- 1 teaspoon dried crushed red pepper
- ½ teaspoon ground cumin

Bring all ingredients to boil in heavy large saucepan, whisking occasionally. Reduce heat to medium-low. Cover and simmer until sauce thickens and flavors blend, whisking often, about 20 minutes. Season with salt and pepper. (*Can be made 1 week ahead. Cover and chill.*)

*Smoke-flavored liquid seasoning is available at specialty foods stores and many supermarkets.

MAKES ABOUT 3½ CUPS

Pork Chops with Mustard-Cornichon Sauce

2 tablespoons (¼ stick) butter

2 tablespoons olive oil

6 1-inch-thick pork loin rib chops (about 12 ounces each)

½ cup water

1 large shallot, minced (about 3 tablespoons)

1 garlic clove, minced

2 tablespoons minced cornichons* (about 4)

1 tablespoon Dijon mustard

¼ cup chopped fresh Italian parsley

Known in France as Côtes de Porc Vigneronnes (Grape Growers' Pork Chops), this provincial dish is typical of the simple yet substantial fare served after a hard day of harvesting grapes. Serve with wilted spinach in cream and a red Burgundy or a Burgundian Pinot Noir.

Melt 1 tablespoon butter with 1 tablespoon oil in each of 2 heavy large skillets over medium heat. Sprinkle chops with salt and pepper. Add 3 chops to each skillet and sauté until lightly browned, about 3 minutes per side. Cover skillets and cook until thermometer inserted into center of chops registers 145°F, about 9 minutes. Transfer chops to warm platter; tent with foil to keep warm.

Add half of water, shallot, and garlic to each skillet. Cook until shallot is soft, scraping up any browned bits, about 2 minutes. Add any juices from chops. Whisk in cornichons and mustard. Season with salt and pepper. Pour over chops. Sprinkle chops with parsley.

Cornichons are tiny brine-packed French pickles, available at specialty foods stores and some supermarkets.

6 SERVINGS

Spiced Chicken with Oranges

 4 skinless boneless chicken breast halves
 2 teaspoons Chinese five-spice powder
 2 teaspoons toasted sesame seeds
 2 tablespoons (¼ stick) butter

 1 medium-size red onion, thinly sliced
 ½ cup orange juice
 3 tablespoons soy sauce
 2 teaspoons hot pepper oil
 2 seedless oranges, peeled and sliced crosswise into ½-inch-thick rounds

Sprinkle chicken with salt, pepper, five-spice powder, and sesame seeds. Melt butter in heavy large skillet over medium heat. Sauté chicken until golden brown and cooked through, about 5 minutes per side. Using tongs, transfer to plate.

Add onion to drippings in skillet and sauté until tender, stirring often, about 3 minutes. Add orange juice, soy sauce, and pepper oil. Reduce heat to medium-low and simmer 2 minutes, stirring often. Add oranges and stir until just heated through, about 1 minute. Return chicken to skillet to reheat if necessary. Divide onion-orange mixture among 4 plates, top with chicken, and serve.

4 SERVINGS

Lemon-Dill Chicken Burgers

  1   pound ground chicken breasts
 ⅓   cup finely chopped onion
 ⅓   cup finely chopped celery
 ¾   cup finely crushed seasoned corn bread stuffing mix
  8   tablespoons olive oil
  4   tablespoons fresh lemon juice
  1   tablespoon chopped fresh dill
  1   teaspoon grated lemon peel
  1   teaspoon salt
 ¾   teaspoon freshly ground pepper

These are terrific on their own or served on a hamburger bun.

Using fork, blend chicken, onion, celery, ¼ cup stuffing, 2 tablespoons oil, 1 tablespoon lemon juice, dill, lemon peel, salt, and pepper in large bowl. Form mixture into eight ½-inch-thick patties. Sprinkle patties with ¼ cup stuffing, pressing to adhere. Turn over and repeat.

Working in 2 batches, heat 2 tablespoons oil in large skillet over medium-high heat. Add patties and cook until brown and cooked through, about 2½ minutes per side. Transfer burgers to plate and tent with foil.

Add 2 tablespoons oil and 3 tablespoons lemon juice to skillet. Bring to boil, scraping up browned bits. Drizzle over burgers.

4 SERVINGS

Chicken Breasts with Tomatoes and Marjoram

 24   ounces cherry tomatoes (about 4 cups), stemmed
 ¼   cup olive oil
  5   garlic cloves, pressed
1¼   teaspoons dried crushed red pepper
  2   tablespoons chopped fresh marjoram
  4   chicken breast halves with ribs

Preheat oven to 450°F. Toss tomatoes, oil, garlic, red pepper, and 1 tablespoon marjoram in large bowl. Place chicken on rimmed baking sheet. Pour tomato mixture over chicken, arranging tomatoes in single layer. Sprinkle with salt and pepper. Roast until chicken is cooked and tomatoes are blistered, about 35 minutes. Transfer chicken to plates. Spoon tomatoes and juices over. Sprinkle with 1 tablespoon marjoram.

4 SERVINGS

Roast Chicken with Herbed Olivada

1½ cups pitted Kalamata olives (about 8 ounces)
4 teaspoons finely chopped fresh rosemary
2 garlic cloves
½ teaspoon dried crushed red pepper
½ teaspoon salt
½ teaspoon freshly ground black pepper
5 tablespoons extra-virgin olive oil

1 7-pound roasting chicken

⅓ cup dry white wine
⅔ cup (about) low-salt chicken broth

Combine olives, rosemary, garlic, crushed red pepper, salt, and black pepper in processor. Blend until olives and garlic are chopped finely. With machine running, add 4 tablespoons oil through feed tube and blend until coarse paste forms. (*Olivada can be made 1 day ahead. Transfer to small bowl, cover, and refrigerate.*)

Position rack in bottom third of oven and preheat to 425°F. Starting at neck end of chicken, carefully slide hand under skin, loosening skin over breast, thighs, and top of drumsticks. Spread olive paste as evenly as possible over meat under loosened skin. Rub outside of chicken with remaining 1 tablespoon oil. Fold wing tips under; tie legs together loosely to hold shape. Place chicken on rack set in roasting pan.

Roast chicken until skin is golden brown and thermometer inserted into thickest part of thigh registers 180°F, about 1 hour 20 minutes. Using carving fork, tilt chicken to empty juices from cavity into pan. Place chicken on platter; tent loosely with foil.

Pour pan juices into 2-cup glass measuring cup; spoon off fat that rises to top. Add wine and enough broth to juices to measure 1⅓ cups. Pour liquid back into same roasting pan. Set pan over 2 burners and boil until sauce thickens and reduces to ¾ cup, scraping up browned bits, about 5 minutes. Season sauce with salt and pepper; pour into gravy boat. Serve chicken with sauce.

6 SERVINGS

Grilled Chicken with Cumin and Coriander

- 1 cup olive oil
- ¼ cup red wine vinegar
- 3 tablespoons ground cumin
- 1½ tablespoons ground coriander
- 2 teaspoons ground cinnamon
- 2 teaspoons salt
- 2 teaspoons sugar
- ¼ teaspoon cayenne pepper
- 4 large chicken breast halves with skin and ribs, cut crosswise in half
- 4 chicken legs
- 4 chicken thighs

- ¼ cup minced fresh parsley

Whisk first 8 ingredients in large glass baking dish. Add all chicken; turn to coat. Cover with plastic wrap; chill 4 to 6 hours.

Prepare barbecue (medium heat). Place marinade-coated chicken on barbecue. Grill chicken until just cooked through, occasionally brushing with any remaining marinade, about 10 minutes per side for breasts and about 12 minutes per side for leg and thigh pieces. Transfer chicken to platter. Sprinkle with parsley.

6 SERVINGS

Chicken with Mustard and Tarragon Cream Sauce

- 1 tablespoon butter
- 1 tablespoon olive oil
- 1 3-pound whole chicken, cut into 8 pieces

- ¾ cup chopped shallots
- ¼ cup brandy
- 1 cup low-salt chicken broth

- ½ cup whipping cream
- 4 teaspoons chopped fresh tarragon
- 2 teaspoons Dijon mustard

In a classic pairing, tarragon brightens up sautéed chicken. Serve with steamed rice to soak up the luscious sauce.

Melt butter with oil in heavy large skillet over high heat. Sprinkle chicken with salt and pepper. Cook, skin side down, until brown, about 5 minutes. Turn over; cook 1 minute. Using tongs, transfer chicken to plate.

Add shallots to same skillet; reduce heat to medium-low. Sauté until soft, about 3 minutes. Add brandy; simmer until liquid is reduced, scraping up browned bits, about 2 minutes. Whisk in broth. Return chicken to skillet, skin side up. Reduce heat to medium-low. Cover and simmer until chicken is cooked, about 20 minutes. Transfer to platter; reserve skillet.

Whisk cream, tarragon, and mustard into same skillet. Increase heat to high; boil until sauce is thickened, about 2 minutes. Season with salt and pepper. Pour sauce over chicken.

4 SERVINGS

Chicken in Green Pumpkin-Seed Sauce

CHICKEN

- 5 cups water
- 6 chicken thighs with skin and bones
- ¼ large white onion
- 3 garlic cloves, halved
- 3 large fresh cilantro sprigs
- 1 teaspoon fine sea salt

SAUCE

- 1⅔ cups shelled pumpkin seeds (pepitas)
- 6 whole black peppercorns

- 12 ounces tomatillos, husked, rinsed, coarsely chopped
- ¼ cup chopped white onion
- ¼ cup chopped fresh cilantro
- 3 medium serrano chiles, chopped with seeds
- 2 garlic cloves, chopped
- 1 teaspoon fine sea salt
- 6 tablespoons corn oil

FOR CHICKEN: Bring all ingredients to boil in large pot. Reduce heat; simmer uncovered until chicken is cooked through, about 30 minutes. Transfer chicken to bowl; cover to keep warm. Reserve chicken broth in pot; spoon off fat from surface.

MEANWHILE, BEGIN SAUCE: Heat heavy large skillet over medium-low heat. Add pepitas; stir frequently until seeds puff and begin to pop, about 15 minutes (do not brown). Transfer to dish; cool. Set aside 2 tablespoons pepitas for garnish. Working in batches, finely grind remaining pepitas with peppercorns in spice mill or coffee grinder.

Puree tomatillos, next 5 ingredients, and ½ cup reserved chicken broth in blender until almost smooth. Heat 2 tablespoons oil in heavy medium skillet over medium-high heat. Add tomatillo mixture and simmer until sauce is thick and reduced to 1 cup, stirring frequently, about 5 minutes.

Heat remaining 4 tablespoons oil in heavy large pot over medium heat. Add ground pepita mixture. Stir constantly until mixture resembles very coarse paste and begins to color in spots, about 9 minutes. Add tomatillo mixture; stir 1 minute. Add 2 cups reserved chicken broth and bring to boil. Reduce heat to medium-low and simmer until sauce is thick, stirring constantly, about 3 minutes longer. Season sauce to taste with salt. Spoon some sauce onto platter. Top with chicken. Spoon remaining sauce over. Garnish with reserved 2 tablespoons pepitas.

6 SERVINGS

Dixie Chicken with Cayenne Spice Rub

- 2 tablespoons salt
- 1 tablespoon coarsely ground black pepper
- 1 tablespoon (packed) golden brown sugar
- 2 teaspoons garlic powder
- 1½ teaspoons cornstarch
- 1½ teaspoons onion powder
- 1 teaspoon lemon-pepper seasoning with garlic and onion
- 1 teaspoon chili powder
- 1 teaspoon cayenne pepper
- ½ cup (1 stick) unsalted butter, room temperature

- 2 4-pound chickens, quartered, rinsed, patted dry

- 1 sourdough baguette, cut on diagonal into ¾-inch-thick slices

Combine first 9 ingredients in small bowl; whisk spice rub to blend well. Transfer 1 tablespoon spice rub to medium bowl; add butter and mix well. (*Rub and seasoned butter can be made 2 days ahead. Cover separately. Chill butter. Bring butter to room temperature before using.*)

Sprinkle spice rub over both sides of chicken pieces. Arrange chicken on waxed-paper-lined baking sheets. Cover with more waxed paper; let stand at room temperature at least 1 hour and up to 2 hours.

Prepare barbecue (medium-high heat). Reserve 4 tablespoons seasoned butter. Spread remaining butter on 1 side of baguette slices. Place bread on platter; cover. Place chicken on grill, skin side up. Grill 20 minutes. Turn chicken over. Grill until skin is deep golden, about 15 minutes. Turn chicken again and grill, skin side up, until cooked through (no red shows when chicken is cut at thigh bone), about 5 minutes longer. Transfer chicken to platter. Brush with reserved 4 tablespoons butter.

Grill bread until golden, 2 minutes per side. Serve toasts with chicken.

8 SERVINGS

Braised Chicken with Leeks and Morels

½	ounce dried morel mushrooms*
1	cup hot water
4	chicken leg-thigh pieces
1	tablespoon olive oil
¾	cup dry white wine
4	leeks (white and pale green parts only), sliced (about 4 cups)
1	cup low-salt chicken broth
1	tablespoon chopped fresh thyme

Place morels in small bowl. Add 1 cup hot water and let stand until morels soften, about 45 minutes. Remove morels and reserve. Strain liquid through fine sieve and reserve.

Season chicken with salt and pepper. Heat oil in heavy large pot over medium-high heat. Add chicken; sauté until brown, about 6 minutes per side. Remove chicken. Add wine; bring to boil, scraping up browned bits. Stir in leeks, broth, thyme, morels, and reserved liquid. Return chicken to pot; bring liquid to boil. Reduce heat, cover, and simmer until chicken is cooked through, turning once, about 40 minutes. Season with salt and pepper. (*Can be made 1 day ahead. Chill uncovered until cold, then cover and keep chilled. Rewarm before serving.*)

*Available at specialty foods stores and some supermarkets.

4 SERVINGS

Backyard Cookout for 8

Spicy Baby Okra and Olives
(*page 14*)

Dixie Chicken with Cayenne Spice Rub
(*opposite; pictured opposite*)

Caesar Coleslaw
(*page 154*)

Grilled Corn

Iced Tea and ***Cold Beer***

S'mores Ice Cream Pie with Warm Milk Chocolate Sauce
(*page 224*)

Grilled Chicken with Garlic and Rosemary

      8   large skinless boneless chicken breast halves
    ½   cup fresh lemon juice
      6   tablespoons Dijon mustard
      1   teaspoon ground black pepper

    ½   cup (1 stick) unsalted butter
    1½ tablespoons finely chopped fresh rosemary
      2   large garlic cloves, minced

Place chicken in 13x9x2-inch glass baking dish. Whisk ¼ cup lemon juice, 4 tablespoons mustard, and black pepper in small bowl to blend. Pour over chicken; turn to coat. Cover; chill at least 2 hours and up to 4 hours, turning occasionally.

Melt butter in heavy small saucepan over medium heat. Add rosemary, garlic, and remaining ¼ cup lemon juice and 2 tablespoons mustard. Simmer basting sauce 5 minutes, whisking occasionally. *(Can be made 4 hours ahead. Let stand at room temperature.)*

Prepare barbecue (medium heat). Rewarm basting sauce; spoon 3 tablespoonfuls into small bowl and reserve. Place chicken on rack. Cover barbecue and grill 2 minutes. Uncover and grill until cooked through, basting occasionally with sauce from pan, about 5 minutes per side. Transfer chicken to platter. Brush with reserved 3 tablespoons sauce.

8 SERVINGS

Roasted Orange-Herb Game Hen

- 2 tablespoons chopped mixed fresh herbs (such as thyme, parsley, and mint)
- 2 tablespoons minced shallots
- 2 teaspoons grated orange peel
- 1 large Cornish game hen, halved lengthwise (about 1½ pounds)
- 1½ tablespoons butter, room temperature
- ½ cup low-salt chicken broth
- ¼ cup orange juice
- 2 tablespoons dry Sherry
- 2 thin orange slices

Preheat oven to 450°F. Mix first 3 ingredients in small bowl. Slide fingertips under skin of hen halves to loosen. Spread ¼ of herb mixture under skin of each hen half. Rub skin with butter; sprinkle with salt and pepper. Place hen halves in shallow roasting pan.

Roast hen halves until golden brown and cooked through, adding chicken broth after 10 minutes and basting twice throughout cooking time, about 30 minutes.

Transfer hen halves to platter. Place roasting pan directly atop burner over medium heat. Add juice, Sherry, and remaining herb mixture; boil until reduced, scraping up browned bits, about 2 minutes. Season with salt and pepper. Spoon sauce over hen halves, garnish with orange slices, and serve.

2 SERVINGS

Pool Party for 8

Chips and Guacamole

Strawberry-Kiwi Sangria with Rose Geranium
(page 41)

Beer* and *Soda

Grilled Chicken with Garlic and Rosemary
(opposite; pictured opposite)

Rice Salad with Feta, Citrus, and Mint
(page 154)

Mixed Green Salad

Almond Crunch Cookies
(page 226)

Watermelon

Spicy Turkey Paella

12 ounces spicy smoked sausage (such as linguiça, andouille, or hot links), cut into
    ½-inch slices

¼ cup garlic-flavored olive oil

2 large yellow onions, chopped

1 large red bell pepper, chopped

2 cups long-grain white rice

¼ teaspoon saffron

4 cups low-salt chicken broth

4 large plum tomatoes, quartered

1 teaspoon salt

1 teaspoon dried oregano

½ teaspoon cayenne pepper

4½ cups cooked leftover turkey, cut into ½-inch cubes

1 cup frozen peas

Preheat oven to 350°F. Brown sausage in large skillet over medium-high heat, about 5 minutes. Remove from heat.

Heat olive oil in 6½-quart pot over medium-high heat. Add onions and cook until golden, stirring often, about 12 minutes. Add bell pepper; cook 3 minutes, stirring frequently. Stir in rice and saffron, then next 5 ingredients. Bring to boil. Reduce heat to medium; cover and cook 15 minutes. Add sausage, turkey, and peas to rice mixture. Bake paella 10 minutes and serve.

6 SERVINGS

Here's a great way to use leftover turkey. Team with a green salad and French bread for a simple and stylish menu.

Southwest Turkey Burgers

1½	pounds ground turkey
½	cup finely crushed tortilla chips (crushed in resealable plastic bag with mallet)
6	tablespoons chopped fresh cilantro
1	tablespoon chili powder
1	teaspoon salt
1	teaspoon ground cumin
½	teaspoon ground black pepper
1	cup purchased chunky salsa
⅓	cup fresh corn kernels

Serve with a black bean salad and burger toppings like pepper Jack cheese, lettuce, and sour cream. Hamburger buns are optional.

Oil grill rack. Prepare barbecue (medium-high heat). Combine turkey, crushed chips, 4 tablespoons cilantro, chili powder, salt, cumin, and pepper in large bowl. Using fork, mix together. Form 6 patties, each about 3½ inches in diameter.

Mix together salsa, corn, and remaining 2 tablespoons cilantro in small bowl. Set aside.

Grill burgers until cooked through, about 5 minutes per side. Divide among plates. Spoon salsa over burgers and serve.

6 SERVINGS

Chipotle Turkey Cutlets with Charred Corn Salsa

1½ cups frozen corn kernels, thawed

1¼ pounds fresh turkey breast fillets
  2 teaspoons chipotle chile powder
  4 tablespoons corn oil

  1 medium-size green bell pepper, diced
  1 small red onion, diced
  ¼ cup chopped fresh cilantro
  1 tablespoon fresh lime juice
    Lime wedges

    Flour Tortillas

Char corn in heavy medium nonstick skillet over medium-high heat, stirring often, about 4 minutes. Set aside.

Sprinkle turkey on both sides with chile powder; sprinkle with salt. Heat 1 tablespoon oil in large skillet over medium-high heat. Add half of turkey and sauté until cooked through, about 1½ minutes per side. Transfer to plate. Repeat with 1 tablespoon oil and remaining turkey.

Add 2 tablespoons oil to drippings in skillet. Add bell pepper and onion; sauté 3 minutes. Increase heat to high and add charred corn. Sauté until peppers begin to brown, about 3 minutes longer. Stir in cilantro and lime juice. Season salsa with salt and pepper; transfer to medium bowl. Return turkey to skillet and reheat, about 1 minute. Spoon salsa over turkey and serve with lime wedges and tortillas.

4 SERVINGS

Roast Duck with Prunes and Juniper Berries

3	cups water
30	juniper berries, slightly crushed
1	5-pound duck; heart, liver, gizzard, and neck reserved
5	large fresh thyme sprigs
1	bay leaf
16	large pitted prunes (about 10 ounces)
2	tablespoons red wine vinegar

Bring 3 cups water, 20 juniper berries, and pinch of salt to boil in large saucepan. Reduce heat to medium; cover and simmer 10 minutes. Set juniper broth aside.

Preheat oven to 450°F. Cut wing tips from duck; reserve. Sprinkle cavity of duck with salt and pepper. Place heart, liver, and gizzard in cavity, then 10 juniper berries, 4 thyme sprigs, and bay leaf. Tie legs together to hold shape. Place duck, breast side up, in roasting pan. Add wing tips and neck to pan. Pour 1 cup juniper broth over duck. Roast duck in center of oven until beginning to brown, about 30 minutes.

Meanwhile, bring remaining juniper broth to boil. Add prunes; cover, reduce heat to medium, and simmer until prunes are soft, about 5 minutes. Using slotted spoon, transfer prunes to small bowl.

Tilt roasting pan; spoon off ½ cup fat from top of liquid. Pour ½ cup prune poaching liquid over duck. Turn duck, breast side down. Pour ½ cup prune poaching liquid over duck. Return to oven; roast 15 minutes. Turn duck, breast side up. Arrange prunes around duck; spoon pan juices over prunes. Drizzle vinegar over duck. Return to oven and roast duck until skin is crisp and juices run clear when thigh is pierced, about 20 minutes longer. Transfer to cutting board, breast side down; let stand 20 minutes.

Discard wing tips and neck. Using slotted spoon, transfer prunes to bowl. Pour pan juices into medium saucepan; spoon off fat. Add thyme sprig. Boil until juices are reduced to 1¼ cups and thickened slightly, stirring occasionally, about 8 minutes. Return prunes to juices to rewarm; season with salt and pepper.

Turn duck, breast side up. Cut legs from duck. Cut off wings with some breast attached. Cut breasts from duck; thinly slice crosswise. Arrange duck on platter. Spoon juices with prunes over and serve.

4 SERVINGS

The juniper berries are an earthy contrast to the sweet prunes in this dish. Serve roasted sliced potatoes and sautéed mushrooms alongside. Pair a red Bordeaux or a varietal blend of Cabernet and Merlot.

Halibut with Oranges, Onions, and Olives

- 3 large oranges

- 3 tablespoons olive oil
- 3 cups thinly sliced red onions
- 3 garlic cloves, thinly sliced
- 1½ 14½-ounce cans diced tomatoes in juice
- 1 cup dry white wine
- ⅓ cup sliced pitted Kalamata olives
- 6 5- to 6-ounce halibut fillets

- 3 ounces drained feta cheese, thinly sliced
- 3 tablespoons chopped fresh chives

Cut off peel and white pith from oranges. Cut oranges between membranes to release segments.

Heat oil in heavy very large skillet over medium-high heat. Add onions and garlic; sauté until tender, about 8 minutes. Add tomatoes and wine. Bring to boil. Reduce heat to medium-low and simmer 3 minutes. Gently stir in orange segments and olives. Season with salt and pepper. Sprinkle halibut with salt and pepper. Arrange in single layer atop vegetable mixture in skillet. Cover; simmer gently until halibut is opaque in center, about 12 minutes.

Spoon vegetables onto plates. Top with halibut. Place cheese atop vegetables. Top with chives.

6 SERVINGS

Tuna Steaks with Herbed Aioli

- ¼ cup olive oil
- 2 tablespoons red wine vinegar
- 2 tablespoons chopped fresh basil
- 2 teaspoons chopped fresh thyme
- 2 teaspoons dried tarragon
- 2 large garlic cloves, finely chopped
- ⅓ cup mayonnaise

- 4 7-ounce tuna steaks (each about 1 inch thick)

SEAFOOD

Whisk together first 6 ingredients in shallow dish for marinade. Place mayonnaise in separate small bowl. Whisk in 1½ tablespoons marinade. Set aioli aside.

Sprinkle fish with salt and pepper. Place fish in marinade in dish, turning to coat evenly. Marinate 1 hour at room temperature, turning fish occasionally.

Oil grill rack. Prepare barbecue (medium-high heat). Grill fish to desired doneness, about 3 minutes per side for medium. Top fish with aioli and serve.

4 SERVINGS

Grilled Whole Fish with Roasted Tomato-Chile Sauce

SAUCE

- 2 pounds ripe tomatoes
- 3 serrano chiles, stemmed
- ¼ cup coarsely chopped white onion
- 3 garlic cloves, chopped
- ¼ cup chopped fresh cilantro
- 1 tablespoon chopped fresh parsley
- 1½ teaspoons fine sea salt

FISH

- 1 3- to 3½-pound whole red snapper, head and scales removed, fish cleaned, butterflied
- ¼ cup canola oil
- 1 teaspoon dried oregano

- 2 teaspoons fresh lime juice
- 12 5- to 6-inch-diameter warm corn tortillas

FOR SAUCE: Line heavy large skillet with foil. Place tomatoes and chiles in skillet; cook over medium-high heat until skins begin to blister and blacken in spots, turning occasionally, about 20 minutes for tomatoes and 10 minutes for chiles. Remove from heat; cool slightly. Peel tomatoes; transfer to processor. Add chiles, onion, and garlic. Blend to coarse puree. Transfer to bowl. Stir in herbs and salt. *(Can be made 4 hours ahead. Cover; chill.)*

FOR FISH: Prepare barbecue (medium-high heat) or preheat broiler. Rinse fish inside and out with cold water; pat dry. Open fish flat, like a book. Rub fish inside and out with oil; sprinkle inside with oregano, salt, and pepper. If grilling, place fish, opened flat, in grill basket. If broiling, place fish, opened flat, on oiled rimmed baking sheet. Grill or broil fish just until opaque in center, about 6 minutes per side.

Using spatula, transfer fish to platter. Sprinkle with lime juice; serve with tomato sauce and warm corn tortillas.

4 SERVINGS

Although you can broil the fish, it is at its best when cooked outside (placing the fish in a grill basket makes it easier to turn over on the barbecue). Ask the fishmonger to remove the head and scales and to clean and butterfly the fish.

Provençal Fish Stew with Rouille

- ¼ cup mayonnaise
- 1 garlic clove, minced
  Pinch of cayenne pepper

  Mediterranean bouquet garni (⅓ cup fennel fronds; 4 thyme sprigs; two 5-inch-long strips orange peel)
- 3 tablespoons olive oil
- 1¾ cups chopped fresh fennel bulb (from 1 large)
- 1 cup thinly sliced leek (white and pale green parts only)
- ½ cup dry white wine
- ¼ teaspoon saffron threads
- 3 cups low-salt chicken broth
- 1½ pounds halibut fillets, cut into 1-inch pieces

- 4 1-inch-thick baguette slices

The bouquet garni for this stew includes orange peel (use a vegetable peeler to make wide strips) and some of the wispy fronds from the top of the fennel bulb that goes into the soup.

Mix mayonnaise, garlic, and cayenne in small bowl. Cover and chill rouille. *(Can be prepared 1 day ahead.)*

Place fennel fronds, thyme sprigs, and orange peel on large square of 2 layers of moistened cheesecloth. Gather cheesecloth and tie securely. Heat 2 tablespoons oil in heavy large pot over medium-high heat. Add fennel bulb and leek and sauté until soft, about 8 minutes. Add wine and saffron; bring to boil. Add broth and bouquet garni; return to boil. Cover, reduce heat to medium-low, and simmer 45 minutes. Add fish; simmer until opaque in center, about 5 minutes.

Meanwhile, preheat oven to 375°F. Brush baguette slices with remaining 1 tablespoon oil. Arrange on baking sheet. Bake until golden brown, about 8 minutes. Spread rouille on toasts. Ladle stew into wide soup bowls, top with toasts, and serve.

4 SERVINGS

Cornmeal-Crusted Trout with Warm Tomato and Tarragon Salsa

½ cup all purpose flour

⅓ cup yellow cornmeal

1 tablespoon ancho chile powder*

1 teaspoon salt

4 12- to 14-ounce whole trout, boned, scaled, heads and tails intact

6 tablespoons olive oil

½ cup chopped red onion

4 garlic cloves, minced

2 teaspoons minced seeded serrano chile

1½ pounds yellow or red tomatoes (preferably vine-ripened), seeded, cut into ½-inch pieces

3 tablespoons bottled clam juice

2 tablespoons fresh lemon juice

2 teaspoons honey

1 tablespoon chopped fresh tarragon

¼ cup shelled pumpkin seeds (pepitas), lightly toasted

Whisk flour, cornmeal, chile powder, and salt in 13x9x2-inch baking dish to blend. Pat trout dry with paper towels. Sprinkle trout cavities with salt and pepper. Coat trout with cornmeal mixture. Heat 2 tablespoons oil in each of 2 heavy large skillets over medium-high heat. Add 2 trout to each skillet and cook until trout are opaque in center and crisp on outside, about 4 minutes per side. Transfer trout to plates.

Wipe out 1 skillet, then heat remaining 2 tablespoons oil in skillet over medium-high heat. Add onion, garlic, and serrano chile. Sauté until onion is tender, about 2 minutes. Add

tomatoes, clam juice, lemon juice, and honey. Cook just until liquids begin to simmer, about 2 minutes. Remove skillet from heat. Stir in tarragon. Season salsa to taste with salt and pepper.

Spoon salsa over trout. Sprinkle with pumpkin seeds and serve.

Ancho chile powder is available in the spice section of most supermarkets.

4 SERVINGS

Catfish Tacos with Avocado Salsa

1	cup chopped plum tomatoes
½	cup chopped peeled avocado
5	tablespoons fresh lime juice
3	tablespoons chopped green onion
3	tablespoons chopped fresh cilantro
3	teaspoons minced jalapeño chiles with seeds
1	pound catfish fillets
2	garlic cloves, minced
4	5- to 6-inch-diameter corn or flour tortillas
2	cups thinly sliced curly leaf lettuce
¼	cup crumbled feta cheese

Preheat oven to 350°F. Mix tomatoes, avocado, 2 tablespoons lime juice, onion, cilantro, and 2 teaspoons jalapeños in small bowl. Season with salt and pepper.

Place fish in single layer on small rimmed baking sheet. Mix garlic, 3 tablespoons lime juice, and 1 teaspoon jalapeños in another small bowl. Drizzle half of lime juice mixture over fish; reserve remainder. Sprinkle fish with salt and pepper; let stand 15 minutes.

Meanwhile, wrap tortillas in foil, enclosing completely. Place in oven until heated through, about 15 minutes.

Preheat broiler. Broil fish just until opaque in center, about 6 minutes. Cut fish into 1-inch pieces. Top each tortilla with ½ cup lettuce, then fish pieces. Drizzle with reserved lime juice mixture. Spoon salsa over; sprinkle with cheese.

4 SERVINGS

Southwestern Lunch for 4

Catfish Tacos with Avocado Salsa
(at left)

Caesar Salad

Lemonade and *Iced Tea*

Mexican Wedding Cookies
(page 228)

Fresh Fruit

Miso-Marinated Salmon with Cucumber-Daikon Relish

¼ cup white miso (fermented soybean paste)*

¼ cup mirin (sweet Japanese rice wine)*

2 tablespoons unseasoned rice vinegar

2 tablespoons minced green onions

1½ tablespoons minced fresh ginger

2 teaspoons oriental sesame oil

6 6-ounce Alaskan salmon fillets, with skin

Nonstick vegetable oil spray

Cucumber-Daikon Relish (see recipe opposite)

1½ teaspoons sesame seeds, toasted

½ cup radish sprouts

½ 8x8-inch sheet dried nori,* cut with scissors into matchstick-size strips

Whisk first 6 ingredients in 13x9x2-inch glass baking dish to blend for marinade. Add salmon; turn to coat. Cover and chill at least 30 minutes and up to 2 hours.

Preheat broiler. Line heavy large baking sheet with foil; spray with non-stick spray. Remove salmon fillets from miso marinade; using rubber spatula, scrape off excess marinade. Arrange salmon, skin side up, on baking sheet. Broil 5 to 6 inches from heat source until skin is crisp, about 2 minutes. Using metal spatula, turn salmon over. Broil until salmon is just cooked through and golden brown on top, about 4 minutes.

Transfer salmon to plates, skin side down. Spoon relish over. Sprinkle with sesame seeds, then sprouts and nori, and serve.

White miso, mirin, and nori (thin sheets of dried seaweed) are available at Japanese markets and in the Asian foods section or refrigerated section of supermarkets across the country.

6 SERVINGS

Cucumber-Daikon Relish

2 English hothouse cucumbers, peeled, halved, seeded, cut crosswise into ¼-inch-thick slices

2 teaspoons sea salt

8 ounces daikon (Japanese white radish), peeled, cut into 2x¼-inch sticks

⅔ cup unseasoned rice vinegar

⅔ cup sugar

1 tablespoon minced fresh ginger

⅛ teaspoon cayenne pepper

Toss cucumbers with sea salt in colander. Place colander over bowl and let stand 15 minutes. Rinse cucumbers. Drain and pat dry with paper towels.

Place radish sticks in medium bowl. Cover with water. Soak 15 minutes. Drain and pat dry with paper towels.

Stir vinegar and next 3 ingredients in large bowl to blend. Add cucumbers and radish; toss to coat. Cover and chill at least 30 minutes and up to 2 hours.

6 SERVINGS

Serve the salmon with steamed white rice tossed with shelled edamame (fresh green soybeans).

Grilled Salmon Fillets with Creamy Horseradish Sauce

SAUCE

- ¾ cup sour cream
- ¼ cup mayonnaise
- 2 tablespoons prepared white horseradish
- 2 tablespoons chopped fresh basil
- 1 tablespoon fresh lemon juice
- 1 teaspoon soy sauce

SALMON

- Nonstick vegetable oil spray
- 3 tablespoons vegetable oil
- 1 tablespoon prepared white horseradish
- 1 tablespoon soy sauce
- 1 small garlic clove, minced
- ½ teaspoon salt
- ¼ teaspoon coarsely ground black pepper
- 6 1-inch-thick salmon fillets (each about 6 ounces)

FOR SAUCE: Mix all ingredients in small bowl. Season with salt and pepper. (*Can be made 1 day ahead. Cover and chill.*)

FOR SALMON: Spray grill rack generously with nonstick spray. Prepare barbecue (medium-high heat). Whisk oil, horseradish, soy sauce, garlic, salt, and pepper in another small bowl. Brush oil mixture over both sides of salmon fillets. Grill salmon just until opaque in center, about 4 minutes per side. Transfer salmon to plates. Serve with sauce.

6 SERVINGS

Sake-Steamed Sea Bass with Ginger and Cilantro

1   cup uncooked medium-grain white rice

¾   cup sake
¾   cup bottled clam juice
1   tablespoon minced peeled ginger
1   garlic clove, flattened
4   5-ounce sea bass fillets
2   large green onions, chopped
4   teaspoons soy sauce
1   teaspoon oriental sesame oil
3   tablespoons chopped fresh cilantro
2   teaspoons sesame seeds, toasted

Cook rice according to package directions.

Meanwhile, combine sake and next 3 ingredients in large skillet deep enough to hold steamer rack. Bring liquid to boil. Reduce heat; simmer 5 minutes. Arrange fish on rack; sprinkle with salt and pepper. Place rack in skillet. Top fish with onions; drizzle with soy sauce and sesame oil. Cover; steam fish until opaque in center, about 5 minutes. Remove steamer rack. Mix cilantro into juices in skillet. Spoon rice onto plates. Top with fish, juices from skillet, and sesame seeds.

4 SERVINGS

Fish on the Grill for 6

Gazpacho with Herbs and Jalapeño
(page 31)

Grilled Salmon Fillets with Creamy Horseradish Sauce
(opposite; pictured opposite)

Watercress, Radish, and Endive Salad with Mustard Seed Vinaigrette
(page 150)

Rice Pilaf

Chardonnay or *Sancerre*

Peaches in Brown Sugar and Rum Sauce with Ice Cream
(page 189)

Seafood Stew with Fennel and Thyme

1½	pounds mussels, scrubbed, debearded
2½	cups chopped onions
1	cup dry white wine
12	parsley sprigs plus ½ cup chopped parsley
2	tablespoons (¼ stick) butter
2	cups finely chopped leeks (white and pale green parts only)
2	cups diced trimmed fennel bulb
4	8-ounce bottles clam juice
4	large fresh thyme sprigs
2	bay leaves
1¾	pounds thick halibut fillets, cut into 1½-inch pieces
10	ounces sea scallops
1	cup crème fraîche*
2	large egg yolks

Combine mussels, 1¼ cups onions, wine, and 8 parsley sprigs in large pot; bring to boil. Cover and cook until mussels open, shaking pot often, about 5 minutes. Using slotted spoon, transfer mussels to large bowl to cool (discard any mussels that do not open). Strain cooking liquid into large measuring cup; discard vegetables in strainer. Add enough water to cooking liquid to measure 2 cups total. Remove mussels from shells if desired.

Melt butter in same large pot over medium heat. Add remaining 1¼ cups onions, leeks, and fennel and sauté until leeks are soft, stirring frequently, about 7 minutes. Add reserved mussel cooking liquid, 4 parsley sprigs, clam juice, thyme sprigs, and bay leaves. Simmer uncovered until vegetables are tender and liquid has reduced by ⅓, about 25 minutes. Add halibut and scallops to broth and simmer until just opaque in center, about 4 minutes. Using slotted spoon, transfer halibut and scallops to bowl. Discard parsley sprigs, thyme sprigs, and bay leaves.

Whisk crème fraîche and egg yolks in medium bowl to blend. Whisk in ½ cup hot cooking liquid from pot. Gradually stir yolk mixture into stew. Cook over medium heat until liquid thickens slightly, stirring constantly, about 5 minutes (do not allow mixture to boil). Return halibut, scallops, and mussels to pan. Cook until halibut is heated through, stirring often, about 5 minutes. Stir in ½ cup chopped parsley. Season with salt and pepper. Serve in warmed shallow bowls.

Crème fraîche is sold at some supermarkets. If unavailable, heat 1 cup whipping cream to lukewarm (85°F). Remove from heat and mix in 2 tablespoons buttermilk. Cover and let stand in warm, draft-free area until slightly thickened, 24 to 48 hours, depending on temperature of room. Refrigerate until ready to use.

6 SERVINGS

Roasted Lobster with Basil-Mint Pesto

2 cups (packed) fresh basil

⅓ cup (packed) fresh mint

4 garlic cloves

⅓ cup olive oil

3 tablespoons pine nuts, lightly toasted

4 1¾-pound live lobsters

2 tablespoons extra-virgin olive oil

⅓ cup freshly grated Parmesan cheese

2 tablespoons whipping cream

2 cups panko (Japanese breadcrumbs)*

1 teaspoon grated lemon peel

Lemon wedges

Preheat oven to 450°F. Blanch basil and mint leaves in large saucepan of boiling water 5 seconds. Drain. Transfer leaves to large bowl of ice water to cool. Drain. Squeeze leaves to remove excess liquid.

Mince garlic in processor. Add basil and mint leaves, ⅓ cup olive oil, and pine nuts. Puree until pesto is smooth.

Drop 1 lobster headfirst into large pot of boiling water. Cover; cook 3 minutes (lobster will not be fully cooked). Using tongs, transfer lobster to work surface. Return water to boil. Repeat with remaining lobsters, 1 at a time. Place 1 lobster, shell side down, on work surface. Place tip of large knife in center of lobster. Cut lobster lengthwise in half from center to end of head (knife might not cut through shell), then cut in half from center to end of tail (use poultry shears to cut through shell if necessary). Crack claws. Repeat with remaining lobsters.

Arrange lobster halves, cut side up, on 2 heavy large baking sheets. Discard head sac and long thin intestinal tract that runs alongside lobster tail meat. Transfer pale green tomalley (liver) from body cavity to pesto in processor. Brush lobster meat with extra-virgin olive oil. Sprinkle meat with salt and pepper.

Blend tomalley into pesto. Transfer to medium bowl. Stir in Parmesan cheese and cream, then panko and lemon peel. Season pesto mixture with salt and pepper; divide among lobster halves, filling cavities and covering meat completely.

Roast lobsters until meat is just cooked through and topping is golden, about 14 minutes. Serve with lemon.

Available at Asian markets and in the Asian foods section of some supermarkets.

4 SERVINGS

Seared Scallops with Garlic-Herb Sabayon

2 heads of garlic
4 teaspoons olive oil

1¼ pounds sea scallops or bay scallops

½ cup bottled clam juice
3 tablespoons dry vermouth
1 tablespoon fresh lemon juice
4 large egg yolks
1 teaspoon chopped fresh parsley
1 teaspoon chopped fresh tarragon
1 teaspoon chopped fresh chives

3 cups lightly packed arugula

Preheat oven to 400°F. Cut top ¼ inch off heads of garlic to expose cloves. Place garlic heads on large sheet of foil. Drizzle 1 teaspoon olive oil over garlic and wrap loosely but completely in aluminium foil; place packet directly on oven rack and roast until very soft, about 45 minutes. Cool. Squeeze garlic from skins into bowl. Using fork, mash roasted garlic until smooth.

Heat 3 teaspoons oil in heavy large skillet over medium-high heat. Sprinkle scallops with salt and pepper. For sea scallops: Sear half at a time until brown and just opaque in center, about 1 minute per side. For bay scallops: Sauté half at a time until opaque, stirring frequently, about 1½ minutes per batch. Transfer to plate. Tent with foil to keep warm.

Meanwhile, bring clam juice and vermouth to boil in small saucepan; remove from heat. Stir in lemon juice. Whisk egg yolks and 2 tablespoons roasted garlic puree in large metal bowl to blend. Gradually whisk in clam juice mixture. Place bowl over saucepan of simmering water (do not allow bowl to touch water) and whisk until sabayon is thick and creamy and thermometer registers 160°F, about 3 minutes. Remove bowl from over water. Whisk in parsley, tarragon, and chives. Season sabayon with salt and pepper.

Divide arugula among 4 warm plates; place scallops atop arugula. Spoon sabayon over scallops and serve.

4 SERVINGS

New England Crab Rolls

6 tablespoons mayonnaise
1 tablespoon fresh lemon juice
1 teaspoon grated lemon peel
⅛ teaspoon cayenne pepper
¾ pound fresh crabmeat, picked over
3 tablespoons finely chopped green onions

2 tablespoons (¼ stick) butter, room temperature
4 hot dog buns, sides split open
4 red leaf or Bibb lettuce leaves

Whisk together mayonnaise, lemon juice, lemon peel, and cayenne pepper in medium bowl. Mix in crabmeat and chopped green onions. Season crab salad to taste with salt and pepper.

Spread butter on insides of hot dog buns. Warm large skillet over medium heat 1 minute. Place buns, buttered side down, in preheated skillet and toast until golden, about 5 minutes. Place 1 lettuce leaf inside each bun. Divide crab salad among buns and serve.

2 SERVINGS

Ginger Shrimp, Sugar Snap Pea, and Corn Stir-Fry

1 pound uncooked large shrimp, peeled, deveined
2 tablespoons canola oil
3 teaspoons minced peeled fresh ginger
2 large garlic cloves, minced
½ teaspoon salt
¼ teaspoon dried crushed red pepper

1 pound sugar snap peas, strings removed
1 cup fresh corn kernels (cut from about 2 ears)
½ cup diced red bell pepper
3 green onions, thinly sliced on diagonal

Mix shrimp, 1 tablespoon oil, 1½ teaspoons ginger, half of garlic, ½ teaspoon salt, and crushed red pepper in medium bowl. Let stand 1 hour.

Heat wok or large nonstick skillet over high heat. Add shrimp mixture; sauté until shrimp are just opaque in center, about 2 minutes. Transfer shrimp to bowl. Add 1 tablespoon oil to wok, then add sugar snap peas, corn, bell pepper, green onions, 1½ teaspoons ginger, and remaining garlic. Stir-fry until vegetables are crisp-tender, about 3 minutes. Return shrimp and any accumulated juices from bowl to wok; stir-fry 1 minute longer. Season with salt and pepper and serve.

4 SERVINGS

Garlic Shrimp

- ¾ cup olive oil
- ½ cup coarsely chopped white onion
- 3 large garlic cloves, chopped
- 1 teaspoon fine sea salt
- ½ teaspoon ground black pepper
- 16 uncooked jumbo shrimp, shells intact, deveined (about 1 pound)

Puree ½ cup oil, onion, garlic, salt, and pepper in blender until almost smooth. Place shrimp in small bowl. Stir in oil mixture. Let shrimp marinate 1 hour.

Heat remaining ¼ cup oil in heavy large skillet over high heat. Add shrimp with marinade and sauté just until shrimp are opaque in center, about 4 minutes. Divide shrimp and marinade from skillet among 4 plates and serve.

4 SERVINGS

Offer this with white rice and a tossed green salad. To devein the shrimp while leaving the shells intact, use kitchen shears or scissors to cut down the center of each shell from the head end of the shrimp toward the tail. Open the shell slightly and remove the vein using the tip of a small, sharp knife.

Coconut Curried Tofu with Green Jasmine Rice

¼ cup unsweetened shredded coconut*

1¾ cups water
1 teaspoon salt
1 cup jasmine or basmati rice

1 cup (packed) coarsely chopped fresh cilantro
¾ cup unsweetened light coconut milk**
4 teaspoons minced fresh ginger
1 tablespoon fresh lime juice
2 large garlic cloves, minced

2 tablespoons vegetable oil
16 ounces extra-firm tofu, drained, patted dry, cut into ½-inch cubes
½ cup thinly sliced green onions
2 teaspoons curry powder
1 teaspoon ground cumin
⅛ teaspoon dried crushed red pepper
1 cup whole small cherry tomatoes

2 tablespoons chopped peanuts

Stir shredded coconut in small nonstick skillet over medium heat until light golden, about 5 minutes. Transfer to bowl.

Bring 1¾ cups water and salt to boil in heavy medium saucepan. Stir in rice; bring to boil. Reduce heat to low, cover, and simmer until water is absorbed, about 18 minutes.

Meanwhile, puree cilantro, ½ cup coconut milk, 1 teaspoon ginger, lime juice, and half of garlic in blender. Mix puree and coconut into rice. Set aside.

Heat oil in large nonstick skillet over high heat. Add tofu; stir-fry until golden, about 6 minutes. Add onions, curry, cumin, red pepper, remaining ginger, and remaining garlic. Stir-fry 1 minute. Stir in tomatoes and remaining coconut milk. Season with salt and pepper.

Divide rice among 4 plates. Top with tofu. Sprinkle with peanuts.

*Available at specialty foods stores and natural foods stores.
**Available at Asian markets and in the Asian foods section of many supermarkets across the country.

4 SERVINGS

Mushroom and Black Bean Burritos

2 tablespoons olive oil
2 medium onions, sliced
2 red bell peppers, cut into strips
3 garlic cloves, minced
10 ounces crimini mushrooms, sliced
10 ounces button mushrooms, sliced
1 tablespoon chili powder
1 15-ounce can black beans, drained
¾ cup purchased tomatillo salsa
½ cup chopped fresh cilantro

6 9- to 10-inch-diameter flour tortillas
6 tablespoons crumbled goat cheese

Heat 1 tablespoon oil in large nonstick skillet over medium-high heat. Add next 3 ingredients; sauté until onions are brown, about 20 minutes. Add remaining oil and all mushrooms; sauté 5 minutes. Stir in chili powder. Sauté until juices evaporate, about 5 minutes. Add beans and salsa; sauté 3 minutes. Add cilantro. Season with salt and pepper.

Meanwhile, preheat oven to 350°F. Wrap tortillas in foil; heat in oven 15 minutes. Place 1 tortilla on each of 6 plates. Spoon mushroom mixture down center of each tortilla, dividing equally. Sprinkle each with 1 tablespoon goat cheese. Fold short ends of tortilla over filling. Roll up, enclosing filling, and serve.

6 SERVINGS

Potato and Green Olive Stew

½ pound cracked green olives
1 tablespoon fresh lemon juice

⅓ cup olive oil
2 cups finely chopped onions
3 pounds small red-skinned new potatoes, peeled if desired, cut into ⅓-inch-thick slices
1¼ teaspoons Hungarian sweet paprika
1 teaspoon ground black pepper
⅛ teaspoon cayenne pepper
1½ cups water
¾ pound plum tomatoes, halved, seeded, diced
Lemon wedges

Combine olives and lemon juice in medium bowl. Let marinate at least 3 hours at room temperature, tossing occasionally. *(Can be made 1 day ahead. Cover and chill.)*

Heat oil in heavy large pot over medium heat. Add onions and sauté 5 minutes. Add potatoes, paprika, black pepper, cayenne pepper, and olives with lemon juice; stir to blend. Add 1½ cups water and bring to boil. Cover, reduce heat to medium-low, and simmer until potatoes are tender, stirring occasionally, about 15 minutes. Mix in tomatoes. Simmer uncovered until flavors blend, about 10 minutes longer. Season stew with salt. Transfer to bowl. Garnish with lemon wedges.

8 SERVINGS

Artichoke, Carrot, and Asparagus Ragout with Fresh Chervil

1 lemon, halved
8 baby artichokes

2½ tablespoons extra-virgin olive oil
1 cup minced red onion
8 ounces baby carrots, peeled, ¼ inch of stem left intact
12 ounces slender asparagus, trimmed, cut into 1-inch lengths
8 ounces sugar snap peas, trimmed, halved crosswise
3 tablespoons chopped fresh chervil

Fill medium bowl with cold water. Squeeze juice from lemon into bowl; add lemon. Cut off stem and top quarter from each artichoke. Bend back dark green outer leaves and snap off at artichoke base until only pale green and yellow leaves remain. Quarter each artichoke.

Using small spoon, scoop out choke and any purple-tipped leaves. Transfer to lemon water.

Heat oil in heavy large skillet over medium heat. Add onion; sauté until soft, about 5 minutes. Drain artichokes; add to skillet along with carrots. Cover; cook until vegetables are crisp-tender, stirring often, about 8 minutes. Add asparagus and sugar snap peas. Cover; cook until vegetables are tender, stirring and adding water by tablespoonfuls if vegetables begin to brown, about 8 minutes. Stir in chervil. Season with salt and pepper.

2 TO 4 SERVINGS

Chervil's delicate anise flavor enhances the baby vegetables. If you don't have chervil, substitute fresh dill. Partner this sensational dish with rice or couscous that has been tossed with toasted pine nuts.

Vegetable and Goat Cheese Tart

CRUST

1½ cups all purpose flour

½ teaspoon salt

6 tablespoons chilled unsalted butter, cut into ½-inch cubes

3 tablespoons chilled solid vegetable shortening, cut into ½-inch cubes

4 tablespoons (about) ice water

FILLING AND TOPPING

5 ounces soft fresh goat cheese

½ cup whipping cream

¼ cup sour cream

⅛ teaspoon salt

Generous pinch of cayenne pepper

3 large eggs

2 tablespoons olive oil

1 small red bell pepper, stemmed, seeded, cut into ½-inch strips

½ medium fennel bulb, cored, cut lengthwise into ½-inch strips

1 small zucchini (about 5 ounces), halved lengthwise, cut crosswise into ½-inch pieces

1 small yellow squash (about 5 ounces), halved lengthwise, cut crosswise into ½-inch pieces

½ cup fresh corn kernels

1 tablespoon chopped fresh basil

Mixed green salad

FOR CRUST: Blend flour and salt in processor. Using on/off turns, cut in butter and shortening until pea-size pieces form. With machine running, add enough ice water by tablespoonfuls to form moist clumps. Gather dough into ball; flatten into disk. Wrap in plastic; refrigerate 1 hour. (*Can be made 1 day ahead. Keep chilled. Soften slightly before continuing.*)

Roll out dough on lightly floured surface to 12-inch round. Transfer to 9-inch-diameter tart pan with removable bottom. Trim dough overhang to 1 inch. Fold overhang in; press to form double-thick sides. Pierce bottom of dough all over with fork. Refrigerate 1 hour.

Preheat oven to 400°F. Bake crust until golden, piercing with fork if bubbles form, about 20 minutes. Cool 5 minutes. Reduce oven temperature to 375°F.

FOR FILLING AND TOPPING: Whisk cheese, cream, sour cream, salt, and cayenne in medium bowl to blend. Add eggs and whisk to blend. Pour into prepared crust. Bake until filling is set, about 20 minutes. Cool 10 minutes.

Meanwhile, heat oil in large skillet over medium heat. Add bell pepper and fennel and sauté until beginning to soften, about 4 minutes. Add zucchini, yellow squash, and corn; sauté until all vegetables are tender, about 12 minutes. Season with salt and pepper. Mound vegetables on top of tart and sprinkle with basil. Serve warm or at room temperature with salad.

6 SERVINGS

Stir-Fried Tofu and Shiitake Mushrooms in Fiery Black Bean Sauce

18 dried shiitake mushrooms
3 cups boiling water

1 tablespoon cornstarch
1 cup vegetable broth
2 tablespoons soy sauce
1 tablespoon rice vinegar
1½ teaspoons sugar
¼ teaspoon coarse kosher salt

3 tablespoons peanut oil
1 small leek (white and pale green parts only), cut into matchstick-size strips
2 tablespoons Asian fermented black beans,* minced
2 tablespoons minced fresh ginger
3 garlic cloves, minced
2 teaspoons chili-garlic sauce*
¼ teaspoon finely crushed Szechuan peppercorns (wild pepper),* or coarsely cracked black pepper
2 14-ounce containers soft tofu, drained, cut into ½-inch cubes

Fresh cilantro sprigs (for garnish)

Place mushrooms in large bowl. Pour 3 cups boiling water over; let soak until mushrooms soften, at least 25 minutes and up to 4 hours. Drain. Cut off stems and discard; finely chop caps.

Dissolve cornstarch in 2 tablespoons vegetable broth in 2-cup measuring cup. Stir in remaining broth, soy sauce, vinegar, sugar, and salt.

Heat oil in heavy large wok or nonstick skillet over high heat until very hot. Add mushrooms; stir-fry until browned, about 3 minutes. Add leek; stir-fry until beginning to brown, about 1 minute. Add black beans, ginger, garlic, chili-garlic sauce, and peppercorns; stir-fry 30 seconds. Stir cornstarch mixture to blend, then stir into vegetable mixture. Add tofu; toss gently to coat with sauce. Reduce heat to low, cover, and simmer until sauce thickens slightly, about 4 minutes.

Spoon tofu mixture into serving bowl. Garnish with cilantro and serve.

Available at Asian markets and specialty foods stores and in the Asian foods section of some supermarkets.

6 SERVINGS

Beefy shiitake mushrooms stand in for the standard ground pork in this version of *ma po* tofu. Team this with rice, green beans, and a Riesling from Alsace or Germany's Rheingau.

Spiced-Up Grilled Cheese

1	6-ounce can tomato paste
3	tablespoons chopped canned chipotle chiles*
1	tablespoon mild-flavored (light) molasses
12	¾-inch-thick slices sourdough bread
18	ounces extra-sharp New York cheddar cheese, thinly sliced
4	plum tomatoes, cut into ¼-inch-thick slices
1	small red onion, thinly sliced
1	cup fresh cilantro leaves
6	tablespoons butter, room temperature

Blend tomato paste, chiles, and molasses in processor until smooth. Spread 1 tablespoon chipotle mixture over 1 side of each bread slice.

Arrange 6 bread slices, chipotle side up, on work surface. Divide half of cheese among bread. Top with tomatoes, then onion, cilantro, and remaining cheese. Top sandwiches with remaining bread, chipotle side down. Spread butter on outside of sandwich tops and bottoms.

Heat 2 large griddles over medium heat. Place 3 sandwiches on each griddle; cook until bread is golden and cheese is melted, about 5 minutes per side.

Canned chipotle chiles in adobo sauce are available at Latin American markets and most supermarkets.

MAKES 6

Tomato and Cucumber Sandwiches with Garlic Butter

¼ cup (½ stick) unsalted butter, room temperature
1 large garlic clove, minced
¼ teaspoon hot pepper sauce
1 tablespoon minced fresh Italian parsley

1 10x8-inch focaccia, cut into 4 equal pieces, each split horizontally
4 medium tomatoes, thinly sliced into rounds
24 thin slices unpeeled English hothouse cucumber
16 thin red onion slices
4 heads of baby lettuce (such as oakleaf) or 4 curly lettuce leaves

Combine butter, garlic, and hot pepper sauce in bowl. Using back of fork, mash until mixture is almost smooth. Season with salt and pepper. Mix in parsley.

Preheat oven to 325°F. Arrange bread pieces, cut side down, directly on oven rack. Bake until bread is slightly crusty, about 5 minutes. Arrange bread, cut side up, on work surface. Spread cut sides with garlic butter. Arrange tomatoes, cucumber, and onion on bottom halves of bread. Top with lettuce, then bread tops. Press to compact slightly. Cut sandwiches diagonally in half.

4 SERVINGS

Bell Pepper and Cheddar Frittata

1 Yukon Gold potato, peeled, cut into ¼-inch cubes
2½ tablespoons olive oil
1 large red bell pepper, chopped
1 large onion, coarsely chopped
4 garlic cloves, finely chopped
3 tablespoons chopped fresh oregano

8 large eggs
1 teaspoon salt
¾ teaspoon coarsely ground pepper
1 cup grated sharp cheddar cheese

Cook potato in saucepan of boiling salted water until tender, about 8 minutes. Drain. Heat oil in large ovenproof skillet over medium-high heat. Add pepper and onion; sauté until tender, about 6 minutes. Add potato, garlic, and oregano; sauté 1 minute.

Whisk eggs, salt, and pepper in medium bowl. Pour over vegetables in skillet. Reduce heat to medium-low, cover skillet, and cook until eggs are set around edges, about 8 minutes. Sprinkle with cheese.

Meanwhile, preheat broiler. Place skillet in broiler 4 to 5 inches from heat source and cook until cheese is melted, about 2 minutes. Let stand 1 minute. Cut into 8 wedges.

4 SERVINGS

Summer Vegetable Stir-Fry with Couscous

    2   cups diced peeled eggplant
1 1/2   teaspoons salt

1 1/2   cups water
    1   cup couscous

2 1/2   tablespoons canola oil
2 1/2   tablespoons red wine vinegar
    1   cup diced peeled carrots
    1   cup diced zucchini
    1   cup diced yellow crookneck squash
    1   cup small broccoli florets
    1   cup diced red bell pepper
  1/2   cup diced red onion
    2   garlic cloves, minced
    4   tablespoons chopped fresh basil
    2   tablespoons chopped fresh mint
    2   tablespoons pine nuts, toasted

Toss eggplant and 1 teaspoon salt in medium bowl; let stand 30 minutes. Rinse and drain eggplant. Pat dry.

Bring 1 1/2 cups water and 1/2 teaspoon salt to boil in large saucepan. Stir in couscous. Remove from heat. Cover; let stand 10 minutes. Uncover; fluff with fork.

Whisk 1 1/2 tablespoons oil and vinegar in small bowl. Heat 1 tablespoon oil in wok or large nonstick skillet over medium-high heat. Add eggplant and carrots; stir-fry 3 minutes. Add zucchini and next 5 ingredients; stir-fry until crisp-tender, about 2 minutes. Add couscous and vinegar mixture; stir-fry 1 minute. Stir in herbs. Season with salt and pepper. Top with nuts.

4 SERVINGS

Brunch on the Terrace for 8

Bell Pepper and Cheddar Frittata
(opposite; double recipe)

Fruit Salad with Tangerine Dressing
(page 155)

Golden Brioche
(page 164)

Assorted Jams

Maple-Pecan Sticky Bars
(page 232)

Coffee and *Tea*

Freshly Squeezed Orange Juice

Skillet Polenta with Tomatoes and Gorgonzola

2 tablespoons extra-virgin olive oil

4 cups water
1⅓ cups yellow cornmeal
1¼ teaspoons salt
½ cup slivered fresh basil

2 cups halved cherry tomatoes
2 garlic cloves, minced
1 cup crumbled Gorgonzola cheese (about 4 ounces)
1 cup shredded mozzarella cheese (about 4 ounces)

Preheat oven to 450°F. Brush 12-inch-diameter ovenproof skillet with 1 tablespoon olive oil.

Combine 4 cups water, yellow cornmeal, and salt in heavy large saucepan. Bring to boil over medium-high heat, whisking constantly. Reduce heat to medium-low and cook until polenta is very thick and pulls away from sides of pan, whisking constantly, about 3 minutes. Whisk in remaining 1 tablespoon olive oil and ¼ cup basil. Transfer polenta to prepared skillet; flatten polenta to even thickness.

Sprinkle polenta with tomatoes and garlic. Sprinkle evenly with Gorgonzola, mozzarella, and remaining ¼ cup basil. Bake until cheese is melted and bubbling, about 16 minutes. Cut polenta into wedges and serve from skillet.

4 SERVINGS

Cannellini and Fennel Salad with Roasted Peppers, Mushrooms, and Zucchini

Nonstick vegetable oil spray
2 large red bell peppers, quartered
2 large portobello mushrooms, stems removed, caps quartered
4 small zucchini, halved lengthwise
1 tablespoon chopped fresh thyme
1 tablespoon chopped fresh mint
2 teaspoons grated orange peel

¼ cup extra-virgin olive oil
¼ cup red wine vinegar
½ teaspoon fennel seeds, crushed
2 15-ounce cans cannellini (white kidney beans), drained
2 cups chopped fresh fennel
½ cup chopped red onion

6 cups mixed baby greens

4 plum tomatoes, cut into wedges

Preheat oven to 400°F. Spray heavy large baking sheet with nonstick spray. Arrange bell peppers, mushrooms, and zucchini on prepared sheet; sprinkle with salt and pepper. Roast until peppers and zucchini are brown in spots, turning twice, about 35 minutes. Sprinkle with thyme, mint, and orange peel.

Whisk oil, vinegar, and fennel seeds to blend in small bowl. Season dressing to taste with salt and pepper. Mix beans, fennel, onion, and all but 1 tablespoon dressing in medium bowl. Season salad with salt and pepper. Spoon salad into center of large platter.

Toss greens with remaining 1 tablespoon dressing in large bowl; arrange greens around bean salad. Place peppers, mushrooms, and zucchini atop greens. Garnish with tomato wedges and serve.

4 SERVINGS

Mexican Scrambled Eggs

⅔ cup purchased fresh salsa

½ cup drained canned black beans

5 tablespoons chopped fresh cilantro

2 tablespoons (¼ stick) butter

5 large eggs

3 tablespoons cream cheese, cut into small pieces

2 purchased taco or tostada shells, warmed

Stir together salsa, beans, and 3 tablespoons cilantro in medium bowl. Season salsa mixture with salt. Set aside.

Melt butter in heavy medium skillet over medium-low heat. Whisk eggs, remaining 2 tablespoons cilantro, and 1 tablespoon water in large bowl. Season with salt and pepper. Pour egg mixture into skillet. Add cream cheese pieces. Cook until eggs are creamy and softly set, stirring constantly, about 5 minutes. Spoon eggs into warmed taco shells. Top with salsa mixture and serve.

2 SERVINGS

Friday Night Dinner and a Movie for 4

Breadsticks with Prosciutto and Arugula
(page 14)

Skillet Polenta with Tomatoes and Gorgonzola
(opposite)

Mixed Greens with Sautéed Bay Scallops
(page 158; halve recipe)

Sauvignon Blanc

Double Banana Split with Rum Whipped Cream
(page 218)

Chilaquiles in Chipotle Sauce

Canola oil (for frying)

18 5- to 6-inch-diameter white corn tortillas, each cut into 8 triangles

Chipotle Sauce (see recipe opposite)

3 fresh oregano sprigs

½ cup chopped fresh cilantro

1 cup crema mexicana or sour cream

1 cup crumbled queso fresco cheese

½ cup chopped white onion

Pour enough oil into large deep skillet to reach depth of 1 inch. Attach deep-fry thermometer; heat oil over medium-high heat to 350°F. Add 12 tortilla triangles at a time to oil. Fry until golden, turning occasionally, about 1 minute. Using slotted spoon, transfer chips to paper towels; cool.

Heat Chipotle Sauce in another large deep skillet over medium-high heat. Add oregano; simmer 2 minutes. Season with salt; stir in chips. Immediately divide among 6 plates. Top with cilantro, then crema, queso fresco, and onion.

6 SERVINGS

Chipotle Sauce

- 1 small white onion, peeled, quartered
- 5 large garlic cloves, unpeeled

- 4 pounds tomatoes (about 15 medium)
- 2 canned chipotle chiles

- 2 tablespoons canola oil
- 1 teaspoon fine sea salt

Line heavy large skillet with foil; heat over medium heat. Place onion and garlic in skillet; cook until onion softens and blackens in spots, turning often with tongs, about 15 minutes. Transfer onion and garlic to medium bowl. Peel garlic.

Place same foil-lined skillet over medium-high heat. Working in 2 batches, cook tomatoes in skillet until tender and skins blister and blacken, turning occasionally, about 20 minutes. Transfer to large bowl; cool and peel. Working in batches, puree tomatoes, onion, garlic, and chiles in blender until smooth.

Heat oil in heavy large deep skillet over medium-high heat. Carefully add tomato puree to skillet (mixture will bubble vigorously). Stir in salt. Reduce heat; simmer gently until sauce thickens slightly, stirring often, about 15 minutes.

MAKES ABOUT 7 CUPS

Spaghetti with Grilled Clams, Prosciutto, and Mixed Greens

½ cup extra-virgin olive oil

4 garlic cloves, chopped

¾ teaspoon dried crushed red pepper

8 large leaves mustard greens, stems cut from leaves and discarded, leaves coarsely torn

4 large leaves Swiss chard, stems cut from leaves and discarded, leaves coarsely torn

4 large leaves collard greens, stems cut from leaves and discarded, leaves coarsely torn

½ pound thinly sliced prosciutto

40 large littleneck clams (about 8¾ pounds), scrubbed

1 pound spaghetti

1 lemon, halved

½ cup chopped fresh parsley

Heat oil in heavy large pot over medium-high heat. Add garlic and crushed red pepper and stir until fragrant, about 30 seconds. Add mustard greens, swiss chard, and collard greens and toss until beginning to wilt, about 2 minutes. Remove from heat. *(Can be prepared 2 hours ahead. Let stand at room temperature.)*

Prepare barbecue (medium-high heat). Grill prosciutto until beginning to crisp, about 1 minute per side. Transfer to plate. Tear each slice lengthwise into 1-inch-wide strips; add to pot with greens. Grill clams in batches, if necessary, until each opens, about 6 minutes (discard any clams that do not open). Transfer clams from grill to pot.

Meanwhile, cook spaghetti in another large pot of boiling salted water until just tender but still firm to bite. Drain, reserving 2 cups pasta cooking water. Add pasta to pot with greens, prosciutto, and clams. Squeeze juice from 1 lemon half over. Add parsley. Toss over medium-high heat until heated through, adding reserved pasta cooking water by $1/2$ cupfuls if dry. Season with salt and pepper and more lemon juice, if desired. Transfer pasta mixture to large shallow bowl and serve.

6 SERVINGS

BLT Bow Ties

1 pound farfalle (bow-tie pasta)

12 bacon slices, cut into 1-inch pieces

1 28-ounce can diced tomatoes, drained

¼ teaspoon dried crushed red pepper

3 cups arugula

1 cup sliced green onions

1 cup thinly sliced fresh basil

¼ cup dry white wine

1 cup (packed) grated fresh Parmesan cheese

Cook farfalle in large pot of boiling salted water until tender but still firm to bite. Drain.

Meanwhile, cook bacon in heavy large skillet over medium-high heat until crisp, stirring often. Using slotted spoon, transfer bacon to paper towels. Pour off all but 3 tablespoons bacon drippings from skillet. Add tomatoes and crushed red pepper to skillet; sauté until tomatoes soften, about 2 minutes. Add arugula, onions, $1/2$ cup basil, and bacon; sauté until arugula and basil just wilt, about 2 minutes. Stir in wine; bring to simmer.

Add farfalle to sauce and toss to coat. Mix in $3/4$ cup Parmesan cheese and remaining $1/2$ cup basil; cook until cheese melts and coats pasta, tossing often, about 2 minutes. Season farfalle to taste with salt and pepper. Sprinkle farfalle with remaining cheese and serve.

6 SERVINGS

Sausage and Cheese Manicotti

12 ounces Italian sweet sausages with fennel seeds (about 3½ sausages)
½ cup finely chopped onion
½ cup dry white wine

1 28-ounce can Italian plum tomatoes with basil
⅛ teaspoon dried crushed red pepper
8 large fresh basil leaves, slivered

2 cups fresh whole-milk ricotta cheese or one 15-ounce container whole-milk ricotta cheese
1 cup ¼-inch cubes mild imported provolone cheese (provola) or sharp domestic provolone cheese
2 tablespoons plus ¾ cup freshly grated Parmesan cheese
¼ teaspoon coarsely ground black pepper

1 pound manicotti (large tubular pasta)

1 tablespoon olive oil

Pierce each sausage several times with tip of knife. Place sausages in heavy large saucepan; add onion. Cover; cook over medium-low heat 5 minutes. Turn sausages over; stir onion. Cover and continue to cook until sausages release some fat and onion begins to color, about 5 minutes. Uncover; increase heat to medium. Add wine and simmer until wine evaporates and onion is golden, stirring often, about 5 minutes. Remove from heat.

Puree tomatoes with juices in processor, then strain out seeds and add puree to pan with sausages. Add crushed red pepper. Simmer very gently over low heat until sauce thickens and reduces to scant 2 cups, stirring sauce and turning sausages occasionally, about 1 hour 15 minutes. Add slivered basil and simmer sauce 5 minutes longer. Using tongs, transfer sausages to plate and cool. Season sauce to taste with salt and pepper.

Place ricotta in medium bowl. Mix in provolone cubes, 2 tablespoons grated Parmesan, and black pepper. Cut sausages into ¼-inch cubes; stir into cheese mixture. Season filling to taste with salt. (*Sauce and filling can be made 1 day ahead. Cover separately and chill.*)

Line baking sheet with foil. Cook manicotti in large pot of boiling salted water until still somewhat firm to bite and about ¾ cooked, about 7 minutes (depending on brand). Using tongs, carefully transfer manicotti from pot to foil-lined baking sheet and cool.

Brush olive oil over bottom of 13x9x2-inch glass baking dish; spread 3 tablespoons sauce over. Using teaspoon, fill each of 12 manicotti with about ⅓ cup cheese-sausage mixture. Arrange stuffed pasta in single layer in prepared dish and spoon remaining sauce over. (*Can be made 2 hours ahead. Cover with plastic wrap; let stand at room temperature.*)

Preheat oven to 350°F. Sprinkle remaining ¾ cup Parmesan atop sauce. Bake manicotti uncovered until heated through and sauce is bubbling on bottom of dish, about 20 minutes. Let manicotti stand 5 minutes and serve.

6 SERVINGS

Penne with Chicken, Arugula, Roasted Tomatoes, and Feta

- 3 12-ounce bags cherry tomatoes
- 2 tablespoons olive oil
- 5 large garlic cloves, chopped
- 3/4 teaspoon dried crushed red pepper
- 2 cups shredded roasted chicken breasts without skin (from purchased roast chicken)

- 8 ounces penne pasta

- 6 cups arugula leaves
- 1/2 cup crumbled feta cheese (about 3 ounces)

Preheat oven to 475°F. Mix cherry tomatoes, oil, garlic, and crushed red pepper on rimmed baking sheet. Sprinkle with salt and pepper. Bake until tomatoes are soft and beginning to brown in spots, stirring occasionally, about 20 minutes. Transfer tomato mixture, including any juices, from sheet to large skillet. Add chicken to skillet and simmer until heated through, about 5 minutes.

Meanwhile, cook pasta in large pot of boiling salted water until tender but still firm to bite, stirring occasionally. Ladle out 1/4 cup cooking water and reserve. Drain pasta; return to pot.

Add tomato mixture, arugula, and reserved 1/4 cup cooking water to pasta; toss over medium heat just until arugula begins to wilt, about 30 seconds. Season to taste with salt and pepper. Transfer pasta to bowl. Sprinkle with feta cheese and serve.

4 SERVINGS

Linguini with Butter, Parmesan, and Pepper

- 1 pound linguini
- 2 cups (packed) freshly grated Parmesan cheese (about 6 ounces)
- 1/2 cup (1 stick) unsalted butter, diced, room temperature
  Freshly ground black pepper
  Fresh Parmesan shavings (optional)

Cook pasta in large pot of boiling salted water until just tender, stirring occasionally. Drain, reserving 1 cup cooking liquid. Return pasta to pot. Add 1/4 cup reserved cooking liquid, cheese, and butter. Toss over medium heat until cheese melts and sauce coats pasta, adding more reserved cooking liquid if dry, about 3 minutes. Season generously with salt and pepper. Transfer to serving bowl. Garnish with Parmesan shavings, if desired, and serve.

4 TO 6 SERVINGS

Summer Tomato and Basil Spaghettini

Pasta Party for 8

Antipasto Platter

Breadsticks

Penne with Chicken, Arugula,
Roasted Tomatoes, and Feta
(opposite; double recipe)

Tricolore Salad

Pinot Grigio

Chocolate-Nut Biscotti
(page 230)

Espresso

2½   pounds plum tomatoes, shallow X cut in skin on side opposite stem
  1   cup pitted Niçois or Kalamata olives, halved
  8   tablespoons extra-virgin olive oil
½   cup thinly sliced fresh basil leaves
⅓   cup chopped shallots

  1   cup coarse fresh breadcrumbs made from crustless French bread

  1   pound spaghettini
  1   8-ounce ball water-packed mozzarella cheese, cut into 1½x¼-inch strips
      Fresh basil sprigs

Bring large saucepan of water to boil. Drop in 3 tomatoes; cook 30 seconds. Using slotted spoon, transfer tomatoes to plate. Repeat with remaining tomatoes. When cool, peel tomatoes starting at X. Cut tomatoes in half horizontally; squeeze out seeds and juice. Chop tomatoes coarsely; transfer to large bowl. Mix in olives, 5 tablespoons oil, sliced basil, and shallots.

Heat 3 tablespoons oil in heavy medium skillet over medium heat. Add breadcrumbs. Sauté until golden, about 5 minutes. Set aside.

Cook pasta in large pot of boiling salted water until just tender but still firm to bite, stirring occasionally. Drain well. Add pasta to tomato mixture; toss to blend. Gently mix in cheese. Transfer pasta to serving bowl. Sprinkle with breadcrumbs; garnish with basil sprigs.

4 SERVINGS

Penne in Country Ragù

    4 tablespoons extra-virgin olive oil
    4 ounces Italian sweet sausage, casings removed
    2 garlic cloves, minced
  1/8 teaspoon dried crushed red pepper
    2 medium carrots, finely chopped
    1 medium onion, finely chopped
    1 celery stalk, finely chopped
    2 cups finely chopped canned whole Italian-style plum tomatoes
    1 cup (or more) low-salt chicken broth
  1/2 cup Chianti or other dry red wine
  1/2 cup chopped fresh basil

   12 ounces penne pasta
    1 cup freshly grated pecorino Romano cheese

Heat 2 tablespoons oil in large skillet over medium heat. Add sausage, garlic, and crushed red pepper; sauté until brown, breaking up with fork, about 6 minutes. Add carrots, onion, and celery; sauté until beginning to brown, about 10 minutes. Mix in tomatoes. Reduce heat, cover, and simmer 15 minutes, stirring occasionally. Add 1 cup broth and wine; simmer uncovered until liquid is slightly reduced, about 15 minutes. Add basil; cover and simmer until vegetables are very tender, adding more broth by 1/4 cupfuls if liquid evaporates too quickly and stirring occasionally, about 40 minutes. Simmer uncovered until ragù thickens to desired consistency, stirring often, about 10 minutes longer. Season lightly with salt and pepper. (*Can be prepared 1 day ahead. Refrigerate uncovered until cold, then cover and keep refrigerated. Rewarm over medium heat before using.*)

Cook pasta in large pot of boiling salted water until tender but still firm to bite. Drain, reserving 1/2 cup cooking liquid. Return pasta to pot. Mix in ragù, 1/2 cup Parmesan cheese, and 2 tablespoons olive oil. Add cooking liquid by 1/4 cupfuls to moisten, if desired. Season with salt and pepper.

Divide pasta among plates. Serve, passing 1/2 cup cheese separately.

2 TO 4 SERVINGS

Spaghetti with Mushrooms, Zucchini, and Tarragon

      Olive oil
  1   pound zucchini, trimmed, diced
  ½   teaspoon dried crushed red pepper
  2   pounds mushrooms, sliced
 2½   tablespoons chopped fresh tarragon
  2   tablespoons chopped fresh parsley
  3   large garlic cloves, minced

 12   ounces spaghetti, freshly cooked
  2   large tomatoes, chopped

Brush large deep nonstick skillet with olive oil; heat over medium-high heat. Add zucchini and crushed red pepper; sauté until beginning to soften, about 3 minutes. Transfer to bowl. Brush skillet again with oil; heat over medium-high heat. Add mushrooms; sauté until brown and tender, adding water by tablespoonfuls as needed if mushrooms stick to skillet, about 18 minutes. Add zucchini mixture, herbs, and garlic; stir 1 minute. Season to taste with salt and pepper.

Add pasta and tomatoes to mushroom mixture; toss to blend, adding water by ¼ cupfuls if mixture is dry. Season with salt and pepper. Transfer to bowl.

4 SERVINGS

Angel Hair Pasta with Broccoli and Herb Butter

½ cup (1 stick) unsalted European-style butter, room temperature
2 tablespoons chopped fresh basil
2 tablespoons chopped fresh Italian parsley
1 garlic clove, minced

2 teaspoons olive oil
8 ounces angel hair pasta
2 cups small broccoli florets
Grated Parmesan cheese

Mix first 4 ingredients in small bowl.

Bring large pot of salted water to boil. Add 2 teaspoons olive oil. Add pasta and cook until almost tender, about 3 minutes. Add broccoli and boil until pasta is tender but still firm to bite and broccoli is crisp-tender, about 1 minute longer. Drain pasta and broccoli; transfer to large serving bowl. Add herb butter and toss well to coat. Season to taste with salt and pepper. Serve, passing Parmesan cheese separately.

2 SERVINGS

Farfalle with Ham and Asiago

1 pound farfalle (bow-tie pasta)
2 pounds thin asparagus, trimmed, cut into 1½-inch lengths

1½ cups diced smoked ham
1 cup dry white wine
1 cup whipping cream
1 cup shredded Asiago cheese
1 cup thinly sliced green onions

Cook pasta in pot of boiling salted water 10 minutes. Add asparagus; boil until crisp-tender and pasta is tender but still firm to bite, stirring occasionally, about 3 minutes longer. Drain in colander.

Meanwhile, heat large skillet over medium-high heat. Add ham and cook until just brown, stirring often, about 2 minutes. Add wine; boil until reduced by half, about 2 minutes. Add cream; bring to simmer. Stir in cheese and ¾ cup onions. Add pasta and asparagus; toss with sauce to coat. Season with salt and pepper. Top with ¼ cup onions.

4 TO 6 SERVINGS

Potato Gnocchi with Chicken Livers and Pancetta

GNOCCHI

- 1 1-pound russet potato
- ½ cup plus 2 tablespoons all purpose flour
- 1 large egg
- 1 teaspoon freshly grated Parmesan cheese
- 1 teaspoon extra-virgin olive oil
- ½ teaspoon grated lemon peel
- ½ teaspoon salt
- ¼ teaspoon ground black pepper

SAUCE

- ½ cup water
- ½ ounce dried porcini mushrooms*
- 4 tablespoons (½ stick) butter
- 2 cups sliced crimini mushrooms (about 4 ounces)
- 1½ cups low-salt chicken broth
- 4 teaspoons Sherry wine vinegar

- 2 ounces sliced pancetta,** chopped
- ½ cup finely chopped shallots
- 1 tablespoon minced fresh Italian parsley
- 1 teaspoon minced fresh sage
- 1 teaspoon minced fresh rosemary
- 5 ounces chicken livers, coarsely chopped

FOR GNOCCHI: Preheat oven to 450°F. Pierce potato in several places with fork. Bake until tender, about 1 hour. Let stand until just cool enough to handle, about 15 minutes. Peel potato. Press potato through ricer or food mill or mash in large bowl. Add flour, egg, Parmesan, oil, lemon peel, salt, and pepper and stir just until blended. Turn dough out onto lightly floured surface; divide into 8 pieces. Roll 1 dough piece between hands and surface to 15-inch-long rope. Cut into ½-inch pieces. Place gnocchi on lightly floured baking sheet. Repeat with remaining dough. (*Can be made 6 hours ahead. Cover and chill.*)

FOR SAUCE: Bring ½ cup water to boil in small saucepan. Remove from heat. Add porcini; let soak until soft, about 20 minutes. Melt 1 tablespoon butter in heavy large skillet over medium-high heat. Add crimini mushrooms; sauté until soft, about 5 minutes. Add porcini and their soaking liquid, leaving behind any sediment in bowl. Cook until almost all liquid evaporates, about 1 minute. Add broth and vinegar. Reduce heat to medium; simmer until reduced to 1 cup liquid, about 4 minutes. Whisk in 3 tablespoons butter.

Heat heavy large skillet over medium heat. Add pancetta; sauté until pancetta is crisp, about 2 minutes. Add shallots, parsley, sage, and rosemary. Sauté until shallots are soft, about 5 minutes. Add liver and sauté just until cooked through, about 5 minutes. Add mushroom mixture. Season sauce to taste with salt and pepper.

Meanwhile, bring large pot of salted water to boil. Add gnocchi and cook until rising to surface, about 2 minutes. Continue cooking 1 minute longer. Drain. Divide gnocchi among plates. Spoon sauce over.

Dried porcini mushrooms are available at Italian markets, specialty foods stores, and many supermarkets.
**Pancetta, Italian bacon cured in salt, is available at Italian markets and in the refrigerated deli case of many supermarkets.*

4 SERVINGS

Macaroni and Blue Cheese with Chives

1	pound spiral tube-shaped pasta
2	tablespoons (¼ stick) butter
¼	cup all purpose flour
2	cups whole milk
1	cup whipping cream
3	cups grated cheddar cheese
1½	cups crumbled blue cheese
1	tablespoon minced fresh chives

Preheat oven to 350°F. Butter 13x9x2-inch glass baking dish. Cook pasta in large pot of boiling salted water until tender but still firm to bite, stirring occasionally, about 8 minutes. Drain.

Meanwhile, melt butter in heavy large saucepan over medium-low heat. Add flour. Cook 1 minute, stirring constantly (do not allow to brown). Gradually whisk in milk and cream. Simmer until mixture thickens slightly, whisking occasionally, about 3 minutes. Reduce heat to low. Add cheddar cheese and 1 cup blue cheese. Whisk until cheese melts, about 2 minutes. Season sauce with salt and pepper.

Add cooked pasta to sauce; stir to coat. Transfer mixture to prepared baking dish. Sprinkle with remaining ½ cup blue cheese. Bake until sauce begins to bubble, about 25 minutes.

Sprinkle with chives and serve.

8 SERVINGS

Fireside Supper for 4

Crostini

Potato Gnocchi with
Chicken Livers and Pancetta
(*opposite*)

Arugula Salad

Sangiovese

Strawberry, Mascarpone, and
Marsala Parfaits
(*page 190*)

Coffee

Lentil Ravioli with Sausage and Yellow Tomato Sauce

TOMATO SAUCE

¼ cup vegetable oil

1 large onion, chopped

4 garlic cloves, chopped

2 anchovy fillets, finely chopped

1½ tablespoons chopped jalapeño chiles with seeds

¼ teaspoon (generous) turmeric

1 large pinch of saffron threads

1½ pounds yellow tomatoes, cored, diced (about 3½ cups)

RAVIOLI

3 tablespoons vegetable oil

½ cup finely chopped onion

¼ cup chopped carrot

¼ cup chopped celery

2 garlic cloves, chopped

1 cup dried French green lentils

2 tablespoons chopped seeded jalapeño chiles

1 teaspoon Hungarian hot paprika

2¾ cups low-salt chicken broth

1 tablespoon Sherry wine vinegar

72 (about) wonton wrappers (from two 12-ounce packages)

2 egg whites, beaten to blend

SAUSAGES

⅔ cup all purpose flour

1 large egg, beaten to blend

1⅓ cups fresh breadcrumbs

1 pound fully cooked smoked sausages (such as cotechino, linguiça, or andouille), cut into ⅓-inch-thick slices

¼ cup vegetable oil

FOR SAUCE: Heat oil in large saucepan over medium-high heat. Add onion and sauté until golden, about 12 minutes. Add chopped garlic, anchovies, jalapeños, turmeric, and saffron. Stir until fragrant, about 1 minute. Mix in tomatoes. Reduce heat to medium-low; simmer until sauce thickens, stirring occasionally, about 15 minutes. Season with salt and pepper. *(Can be made 1 day ahead. Cover; refrigerate.)*

FOR RAVIOLI: Heat 3 tablespoons oil in medium saucepan over medium-high heat. Add onion and sauté until brown, about 8 minutes. Add carrot, celery, and garlic; sauté until vegetables begin to color, about 5 minutes. Add lentils, jalapeños, and paprika; stir to coat. Add broth and vinegar and bring to boil. Cover, reduce heat to medium, and simmer until lentils are almost tender, about 1 hour. Uncover and cook until all broth is absorbed, about 25 minutes longer. Season lentil mixture with salt and pepper. Using potato masher, mash mixture coarsely. Transfer filling to medium bowl and chill until cold, about 30 minutes.

Line 2 large baking sheets with foil or parchment paper. Working with 2 wonton wrappers at a time, brush each with egg white. Place 1 tablespoon filling in center of 1 wrapper. Top with second wrapper, egg white side down, and seal, pressing out any air. Cut into round with fluted pastry wheel or 2¾-inch-diameter scalloped cookie cutter, if desired. Place on prepared sheet. Repeat with remaining wrappers and filling. *(Can be made 1 day ahead. Cover tightly and refrigerate.)*

FOR SAUSAGES: Place flour in 1 small bowl, egg in second small bowl, and breadcrumbs in third small bowl. Dip sausage slices into flour, then egg, then crumbs to coat. Place on large plate. *(Can be made 1 day ahead. Cover; chill.)*

Preheat oven to 250°F. Heat ¼ cup vegetable oil in heavy large skillet over medium heat. Add sausages. Sauté until golden, about 4 minutes per side. Place on baking sheet; keep warm in oven.

Bring large pot of generously salted water to boil. Cook ⅓ of ravioli until just tender but still firm to bite, about 5 minutes. Using slotted spoon, divide ravioli between 2 shallow bowls; tent with foil to keep warm. Repeat with remaining ravioli in 2 more batches. Rewarm sauce; spoon around ravioli. Top with sausage.

6 SERVINGS

Tortelloni with Mushroom-Sage Sauce

2 packages (about 9 ounces each) mushroom and cheese tortelloni

¼ cup (½ stick) butter

½ cup chopped shallots

12 ounces fresh shiitake mushrooms, stemmed, caps thickly sliced

1¼ cups dry vermouth or dry white wine

¾ cup whipping cream

1½ tablespoons chopped fresh sage

Cook pasta in pot of boiling salted water according to package directions; drain.

Melt butter in heavy large skillet over medium-high heat. Add shallots; sauté 1 minute. Add mushrooms; sauté until brown, about 7 minutes. Add vermouth and cream. Boil until sauce thickens and coats spoon, about 5 minutes. Stir in sage. Season with salt and pepper. Add pasta; toss until heated through and serve.

6 SERVINGS

Lavash Vegetarian Pizza

- 1 soft lavash bread
- 3 tablespoons olive oil

- ½ cup minced pitted Kalamata olives
- 1 cup grated Monterey Jack cheese
- 1¾ cups crumbled feta cheese
- 1½ cups sliced mushrooms
- 1 cup diced green bell pepper
- ½ cup diced red onion
- 1 cup diced seeded plum tomatoes

Preheat broiler. Place lavash on large baking sheet; brush with 1½ tablespoons oil. Broil until lavash just begins to crisp, about 1 minute.

Reduce oven temperature to 450°F. Turn lavash over on baking sheet, broiled side down. Brush with remaining 1½ tablespoons oil. Spread with olives; sprinkle with Monterey Jack cheese and feta cheese, then mushrooms, onion, bell pepper, and tomatoes. Sprinkle with salt and pepper. Bake until pizza is heated through and cheeses melt, about 10 minutes. Cut into squares.

6 SERVINGS

Look for soft lavash—a large, thin rectangular bread (about 18x12 inches)—in Middle Eastern markets or in the bread section of most supermarkets. Two 11- to 12-inch-diameter flour tortillas can be substituted.

Rustic Green Pepper and Olive Pan Pizza

- 2 tablespoons extra-virgin olive oil
- 1 10-ounce tube refrigerated pizza dough, rolled to 12-inch square
- 1 garlic clove, minced
- 1 8-ounce package shredded pizza blend cheese
- 1 small green bell pepper, thinly sliced
- 1 small red onion, thinly sliced
- ⅓ cup sliced black olives
- 1 tablespoon chopped fresh marjoram

Preheat oven to 400°F. Heat oil in medium ovenproof skillet over medium-high heat. Ease dough into skillet (dough will extend partially up sides). Cook until golden on bottom, about 4 minutes. Turn dough over. Top with remaining ingredients. Transfer skillet to oven; bake until cheese melts and toppings are hot, about 10 minutes. Cut into quarters and serve.

2 SERVINGS

Pizza Bianca with Prosciutto, Arugula, and Parmesan

    2 10-ounce cans refrigerated pizza dough
    4 tablespoons extra-virgin olive oil
   16 thin slices prosciutto (about 6 ounces)
    2 cups (packed) arugula leaves
    2 cups fresh Parmesan shavings (about 4 ounces)

Preheat oven to 500°F. Flour 2 large baking sheets. Unroll each pizza dough on work surface.

TO MAKE ROUND PIZZAS: Cut corners off dough, forming total of two 10-inch rounds.

TO MAKE RECTANGULAR PIZZAS: Cut each crosswise in half to make total of four 8x5-inch rectangles. Arrange on prepared sheets. Drizzle each round pizza with 1 tablespoon olive oil or each rectangular pizza with ½ tablespoon olive oil. Bake until crusts are brown, about 8 minutes. Using metal spatula, loosen crusts from baking sheets. Cut round pizzas in half. Transfer pizza crusts to plates. Top each with prosciutto, arugula, and Parmesan, dividing equally. Drizzle each with ½ tablespoon olive oil and serve immediately.

4 SERVINGS

Grilled Pizza with Tomato, Mozzarella, and Basil

    1 cup diced seeded tomatoes (about 8 ounces)
 1½ cups grated mozzarella cheese (about 6 ounces)
   ½ cup thinly sliced green onions
   ½ cup thinly sliced fresh basil
    2 tablespoons olive oil
    2 tablespoons balsamic vinegar
    2 large garlic cloves, minced

    1 10-ounce tube refrigerated pizza dough
   ¼ cup grated Parmesan cheese

Mix together first 7 ingredients in medium bowl. Let tomato mixture stand 15 to 30 minutes at room temperature.

Oil grill rack. Prepare barbecue (medium-high heat).

Unroll dough onto work surface, stretching to form 12x12-inch square. Cut into 4 equal pieces. Using large spatula, transfer dough to grill rack; cover and grill until bottoms are brown, about 4 minutes. Turn squares over and immediately top each with tomato mixture, leaving ½-inch border. Cover and grill until pizza bottoms are brown and cheese is melted, about 4 minutes. Sprinkle pizzas with Parmesan and serve.

2 SERVINGS

Sweet-and-Sour Radicchio (page 149)

On the Side

Side Dishes

Salads

Breads

Roasted Sugar Snap Peas with Fleur de Sel

1 pound sugar snap peas
1 tablespoon olive oil
  Fleur de sel
2 tablespoons chopped fresh chives

Preheat broiler. Line large baking sheet with foil. Toss peas with oil on prepared baking sheet. Spread peas in single layer. Broil until just crisp-tender and beginning to brown in spots, stirring once with spatula, about 2 minutes. Transfer to bowl. Sprinkle with fleur de sel, then chives, and serve.

6 SERVINGS

White Rice and Wild Rice Pilaf with Tomatoes and Basil

½ cup (1 stick) butter
2 onions, finely chopped
3 garlic cloves, chopped
1½ teaspoons dried oregano
1 cup wild rice, rinsed
7 cups water
1½ cups long-grain white rice
¾ cup chopped green onions
¾ cup chopped fresh basil
1½ pounds plum tomatoes, seeded, chopped (about 3 cups)

Melt ¼ cup butter in heavy large pot over medium heat. Add onions, garlic, and oregano. Cover; cook until onions are soft, stirring often, about 8 minutes. Mix in wild rice. Add 7 cups water; bring to boil, stirring often. Reduce heat to medium-low. Cover; simmer 30 minutes. Mix in white rice. Cover; cook until rice is tender, about 18 minutes. Uncover; simmer until water cooks away, about 4 minutes. Add green onions, basil, and remaining ¼ cup butter. Season with salt and pepper. Mix in tomatoes.

SIDE DISHES

10 SERVINGS

Cider-Glazed Root Vegetables

3 tablespoons butter

12 ounces carrots (about 2 large), peeled, cut into 2x⅓-inch sticks

12 ounces parsnips (about 3 large), peeled, cut into 2x⅓-inch sticks

12 ounces rutabagas (about 2 medium), peeled, cut into 2x⅓-inch sticks

1 cup sparkling apple cider

2 tablespoons Calvados (apple brandy) or other brandy

1 tablespoon minced fresh parsley

Elegant batons of carrots, parsnips, and rutabagas make a pretty presentation. Serve this alongside roast pork, beef, or lamb.

Preheat oven to 425°F. Using ½ tablespoon butter, generously coat 17x12x1-inch heavy rimmed baking sheet. Arrange carrots, parsnips, and rutabagas in single layer on baking sheet. Drizzle cider over vegetables. Dot with remaining 2½ tablespoons butter. Sprinkle with salt and pepper. Cover tightly with foil and bake until vegetables are almost crisp-tender, about 25 minutes. Stir vegetables to coat with juices. Bake uncovered until vegetables are tender and juices are almost evaporated, about 20 minutes. Drizzle Calvados over vegetables and toss to coat.

Transfer mixture to serving bowl. Toss with parsley. Season to taste with salt and pepper and serve immediately.

6 SERVINGS

Herbed Roasted Winter Vegetables

Nonstick vegetable oil spray

3 tablespoons butter

¼ cup olive oil

3 large red beets, peeled, each cut into 6 wedges

2 tablespoons chopped fresh thyme

2 tablespoons chopped fresh summer savory

8 large shallots, peeled, halved through root end

3 large golden beets, peeled, each cut into 6 wedges

2 acorn squash (about 2¾ pounds total), unpeeled, halved, seeded, each half cut into 6 wedges

2 medium turnips, peeled, each cut into 6 wedges

2 large parsnips, peeled, each cut crosswise into 6 pieces

1 large rutabaga, peeled, cut into 12 wedges

12 garlic cloves, peeled

Position 1 rack in top third and 1 rack in bottom third of oven and preheat to 375°F. Spray 2 large rimmed baking sheets with nonstick spray. Melt butter with olive oil in small saucepan over medium-low heat. Combine red beets, large pinch of thyme, large pinch of savory, and 1 tablespoon melted butter mixture in medium bowl. Sprinkle with salt and pepper and toss to coat. Turn beets out onto 1 side of 1 prepared sheet. Combine all remaining vegetables and herbs, garlic, and remaining butter mixture in large bowl. Sprinkle generously with salt and pepper and toss to coat. Divide vegetable mixture between prepared baking sheets.

Roast vegetables 30 minutes. Reverse baking sheets and continue to roast until all vegetables are tender, stirring occasionally, about 45 minutes longer. *(Can be prepared 4 hours ahead. Let stand at room temperature. Rewarm in 350°F oven about 20 minutes.)* Transfer to platter.

12 SERVINGS

Mashed Potatoes with Watercress and Green Onions

2 large bunches watercress, thick stems trimmed

6 pounds russet potatoes, peeled, cut into 2-inch pieces

1½ cups whole milk

½ cup (1 stick) butter

¼ cup olive oil

2 bunches green onions, finely chopped (about 1½ cups)

Bring medium saucepan of water to boil. Add watercress and blanch 10 seconds. Drain. Pat dry and chop watercress.

Cook potatoes in large pot of boiling salted water until very tender, about 25 minutes. Drain. Return potatoes to pot. Stir over medium heat until any excess liquid evaporates, about 2 minutes.

Bring milk almost to simmer in small saucepan. Add hot milk, butter, and oil to potatoes; mash until almost smooth. *(Can be prepared 2 hours ahead. Let stand uncovered at room temperature. Rewarm over medium-low heat, stirring often, before continuing.)* Stir in green onions and watercress. Season with salt and pepper.

12 SERVINGS

Celebration Dinner for 12

Baguettes with Smoked Salmon and Dill Butter
(page 19)

Champagne

Prime Rib

Mashed Potatoes with Watercress and Green Onions
(at left)

Twice-Cooked Beets in Chianti Glaze
(page 149; double recipe)

Cabernet Sauvignon

Mascarpone Cheesecake with Candied Pecans and Dulche de Leche Sauce
(page 196)

Skillet Corn on the Cob with Parmesan and Cilantro

- 4 ears of fresh corn
- 6 tablespoons olive oil
- ⅓ cup freshly grated Parmesan cheese
- 1 garlic clove, minced
- 1 tablespoon fresh lime juice
- 1 teaspoon ground cumin
- ½ teaspoon hot pepper sauce
- ¼ cup chopped fresh cilantro

Cook corn in pot of boiling salted water until tender, about 5 minutes. Drain.

Whisk 5 tablespoons oil, cheese, garlic, lime juice, cumin, and pepper sauce in medium bowl to blend. Season to taste with salt and pepper. Heat remaining 1 tablespoon oil in large skillet over medium-high heat. Add corn and sauté until heated through, turning frequently, about 2 minutes. Brush corn with some of Parmesan mixture. Turn corn and brush with more cheese mixture. Cook until coating begins to color, about 3 minutes. Transfer corn to platter. Mix cilantro into any remaining Parmesan mixture and brush over corn.

4 SERVINGS

Braised Escarole with Currants and Pine Nuts

- 3 tablespoons dried currants
- 2 tablespoons water
- 2 pounds escarole, halved lengthwise, cored, cut crosswise into 2-inch-wide strips
- 3 tablespoons extra-virgin olive oil
- 4 garlic cloves, thinly sliced
- 3 tablespoons pine nuts, toasted

This lovely side dish is delicious with roast pork or chicken, or grilled sausages or fish.

Combine currants and water in small bowl. Let stand 30 minutes. Drain. Transfer currants to medium bowl.

Cook escarole in batches in large pot of boiling water just until wilted, about 2 minutes. Drain; cool under cold running water. Drain again; squeeze to remove excess water. Combine with currants.

Heat oil in large skillet over medium-high heat. Add garlic; sauté just until beginning to color, about 2 minutes. Add escarole mixture and pine nuts. Sprinkle with salt and pepper. Sauté until escarole is heated through, about 5 minutes. Season with salt and pepper.

6 SERVINGS

Potatoes Roasted with Olive Oil and Bay Leaves

8	medium-size red-skinned potatoes
½	cup olive oil
40	small bay leaves
1	tablespoon coarse sea salt
2	teaspoons herbes de Provence*
1½	teaspoons coarsely cracked black pepper

Preheat oven to 350°F. Using small sharp knife and working on 1 potato, make 5 crosswise vertical cuts, spaced evenly apart, from 1 side to other side (do not cut through). Place potato in 13x9x2-inch broilerproof baking dish. Repeat with remaining potatoes. Add some of oil to dish and toss potatoes to coat. Slide 1 bay leaf into each cut in each potato. Mix salt, herbs, and pepper in small bowl and sprinkle over potatoes. Roast potatoes until tender, about 55 minutes. Remove dish from oven. Preheat broiler. Drizzle remaining oil over potatoes. Broil until potatoes begin to brown, about 4 minutes.

A dried herb mixture available at specialty foods stores and in the spice section of some supermarkets. A combination of dried thyme, basil, savory, and fennel seeds can be substituted.

6 SERVINGS

Herbed Quinoa Pilaf

4	cups quinoa (about 18 ounces)
4½	cups water
¾	teaspoon salt
3	tablespoons extra-virgin olive oil
1 ½	tablespoons fresh lemon juice
1½	cups pine nuts, lightly toasted
¾	cup finely chopped red onion
1½	cups chopped fresh basil

Place quinoa in large strainer. Rinse under cold running water until water is clear. Transfer quinoa to large saucepan; add 4½ cups water and salt. Bring to boil. Reduce heat to medium-low, cover, and simmer until water is absorbed and quinoa is tender, about 20 minutes. Transfer quinoa to large bowl; fluff with fork. Stir in oil and lemon juice. Cool to room temperature. Mix in pine nuts and red onion. Season with salt and pepper. *(Can be prepared 6 hours ahead. Cover and chill.)* Mix in basil.

12 SERVINGS

Wok-Seared Sesame Green Beans

1½ pounds green beans, trimmed

1½ tablespoons oriental sesame oil

3 tablespoons soy sauce

1½ tablespoons rice vinegar

1½ tablespoons (packed) golden brown sugar

¼ teaspoon ground black pepper

2 tablespoons sesame seeds, toasted

Cook green beans in large pot of boiling water until crisp-tender, about 3 minutes. Drain. Transfer green beans to large bowl of ice water to cool. Drain again. Pat green beans dry. *(Can be prepared 1 day ahead. Wrap green beans in paper towels and enclose in resealable plastic bag. Refrigerate.)*

Heat oil in heavy large wok or nonstick skillet over high heat. Add green beans and stir-fry until heated through, about 2 minutes. Add soy sauce, rice vinegar, sugar, and pepper. Stir-fry until sauce reduces slightly and loosely coats green beans, about 2 minutes longer. Add sesame seeds and toss to coat. Transfer green bean mixture to bowl and serve.

6 SERVINGS

Roasted Brussels Sprouts with Balsamic Vinegar and Pancetta

    2 tablespoons olive oil
    2 pounds brussels sprouts, trimmed, halved
    6 ounces thinly sliced pancetta* or bacon, chopped
    2 garlic cloves, finely chopped

    3 tablespoons balsamic vinegar
    1 tablespoon chopped fresh thyme

Preheat oven to 450°F. Brush heavy large rimmed baking sheet with 1 tablespoon oil. Place 1 tablespoon oil in large bowl; mix in brussels sprouts, pancetta, and garlic. Sprinkle with salt and pepper. Spread mixture in single layer on prepared sheet. Roast until brussels sprouts are tender and brown, stirring often, about 20 minutes. (*Can be made 3 hours ahead. Let stand at room temperature.*)

Drizzle brussels sprouts with vinegar; sprinkle with thyme. Stir to coat. Return to 450°F oven; roast until heated through, about 5 minutes. Transfer to bowl; serve.

Pancetta, Italian bacon cured in salt, is available at Italian markets and in the refrigerated deli case of many supermarkets.

8 TO 10 SERVINGS

Roasted Yams with Citrus and Coriander Butter

- 1 tablespoon coriander seeds
- ¼ cup (½ stick) butter, room temperature
- 1 tablespoon golden brown sugar
- 1 tablespoon grated orange peel
- 1½ teaspoons grated lemon peel

  Nonstick vegetable oil spray
- 3 pounds long narrow yams (red-skinned sweet potatoes), unpeeled, halved lengthwise, cut crosswise into ½-inch-thick slices
- 1½ tablespoons olive oil

- 2 tablespoons minced fresh Italian parsley

Stir coriander seeds in small skillet over medium-high heat until darkened in color and fragrant, about 4 minutes. Cool seeds; grind in spice mill or enclose in plastic bag and crush finely with mallet. Place seeds in small bowl. Mix in butter, sugar, orange peel, and lemon peel. Season butter with salt and pepper. *(Can be made 1 week ahead. Cover and chill.)*

Position rack in bottom third of oven and preheat to 375°F. Spray heavy large rimmed baking sheet with nonstick spray. Toss yams and olive oil in large bowl to coat. Spread yams in single layer on prepared sheet. Sprinkle with salt and pepper. Roast until tender and

golden brown, stirring occasionally, about 30 minutes. *(Can be made 1 day ahead. Cover and refrigerate on sheet.)*

Drop butter onto yams in small dollops. Roast until heated through, glazed, and browned, stirring occasionally, about 20 minutes (or 25 minutes if refrigerated). Season with salt and pepper. Mound in bowl; sprinkle with parsley.

10 SERVINGS

Sweet-and-Sour Radicchio

- 2 tablespoons unsalted butter
- 2 tablespoons olive oil
- 1 large onion, thinly sliced
- 2 tablespoons sugar
- ½ cup apple cider vinegar
- 2 large heads of radicchio (about 1½ pounds), cored, each cut into 8 wedges
- ⅓ cup raisins
- 1½ teaspoons salt
- ½ teaspoon ground black pepper
- 2 tablespoons toasted pine nuts

The radicchio is seasoned in the style of a Sicilian *agrodolce* ("sour-sweet") dish, which typically combines a vegetable with raisins, pine nuts, vinegar, and a sweetener.

Melt butter with oil in heavy large skillet over medium-high heat. Add onion and sugar. Sauté until onion is lightly browned, about 7 minutes. Add vinegar; stir to blend. Add radicchio, raisins, salt, and pepper. Cook until radicchio is just wilted, about 5 minutes. Transfer to serving dish; sprinkle with pine nuts.

6 SERVINGS

Twice-Cooked Beets in Chianti Glaze

- 8 2½-inch-diameter beets, trimmed, scrubbed
- 4 tablespoons extra-virgin olive oil
- 2 medium leeks (white and pale green parts only), trimmed, halved lengthwise, thinly sliced (about 3 cups)
- 2 cups Chianti or other dry red wine
- 2 tablespoons (¼ stick) butter

The wine glaze both balances the natural sweetness of the beets and intensifies the savory beet flavor. In Tuscany, this is a favorite side dish for game and fowl.

Preheat oven to 450°F. Toss beets with 2 tablespoons oil in 13x9x2-inch glass baking dish. Roast beets uncovered until tender when pierced with knife, about 1 hour. Cool beets slightly, then slip off peel. Cut beets into quarters.

Heat remaining 2 tablespoons oil in heavy large skillet over medium heat. Add leeks and sauté until translucent and tender, about 12 minutes. Add beets; sprinkle with salt and pepper. Sauté 5 minutes. Add Chianti and bring to boil. Reduce heat to medium and simmer until wine almost evaporates and glaze coats beets, stirring occasionally, about 15 minutes. Add butter and stir until melted. Season to taste with salt and pepper. Transfer to bowl and serve.

6 SERVINGS

Watercress, Radish, and Endive Salad with Mustard Seed Vinaigrette

1½ teaspoons mustard seeds
2 tablespoons apple cider vinegar
1 tablespoon fresh lemon juice
1 teaspoon Dijon mustard
⅓ cup olive oil

2 bunches watercress, thick stems trimmed (about 8 cups)
2 small heads of Belgian endive, cut lengthwise into ¼-inch-wide strips
2 bunches radishes, trimmed, sliced

SALADS Stir mustard seeds in small dry skillet over medium heat until seeds begin to pop, about 3 minutes. Transfer to small bowl; cool. Add vinegar, lemon juice, and Dijon mustard to mustard seeds. Gradually whisk in oil. Season dressing with salt and pepper.

Toss watercress, endive, and radishes in bowl with enough dressing to coat.

6 SERVINGS

Romaine Salad with Chipotle Dressing and Warm Queso Fresco

⅓ cup plus 3 tablespoons extra-virgin olive oil
2 teaspoons bottled chipotle hot sauce
½ teaspoon sugar

2 cups cornflakes, finely crumbled
2 teaspoons dried oregano
1 12-ounce round Mexican queso fresco cheese, cut into 12 wedges

1 very large head of romaine lettuce, torn into bite-size pieces

Chipotle hot sauce and *queso fresco* can be found at Latin American markets and at many supermarkets.

Whisk ⅓ cup oil, hot sauce, and sugar in small bowl to blend. Season dressing to taste with salt and pepper.

Brush baking sheet with olive oil. Mix cornflakes and oregano in medium bowl. Sprinkle with salt and pepper. Brush cheese wedges on all sides with 3 tablespoons oil. Dip cheese wedges in cornflake mixture, coating completely. Place on prepared baking sheet. (*Dressing and cheese wedges can be made 4 hours ahead. Let dressing stand at room temperature; cover and chill cheese.*)

Preheat oven to 400°F. Bake cheese wedges until hot and softened but not melted, about 5 minutes.

Meanwhile, toss lettuce with dressing in large bowl. Divide among 6 plates. Top each salad with 2 hot cheese wedges.

6 SERVINGS

Heirloom Tomato Salad with Blue Cheese

8 ½-inch-thick slices crusty bread
4 large garlic cloves, halved
3 tablespoons plus ⅓ cup extra-virgin olive oil
1 cup currant or grape tomatoes or halved cherry or pear tomatoes
½ cup chopped green onions

10 medium heirloom tomatoes of assorted colors, cored, thinly sliced
1 small red onion, sliced paper-thin
3 celery stalks, sliced thin on diagonal
1½ cups coarsely crumbled blue cheese

Prepare barbecue (medium-high heat). Rub bread with cut garlic halves; brush bread with 3 tablespoons oil. Combine remaining ⅓ cup oil, currant tomatoes, and green onions in medium bowl; toss to coat. Season with salt and pepper.

Overlap tomato slices in concentric circles on platter, alternating colors. Scatter onion and celery slices over tomatoes. Sprinkle with salt and pepper. Spoon tomato and green onion mixture over. Sprinkle with crumbled cheese.

Grill bread until golden brown, about 2 minutes per side. Cut each slice diagonally in half; serve with salad.

6 TO 8 SERVINGS

Garden Salad with Pears and Pine Nuts

¼ cup olive oil
¼ cup canola oil or vegetable oil
3 tablespoons fresh lemon juice
2 tablespoons red wine vinegar
1 tablespoon honey
1 tablespoon chopped fresh thyme
1 tablespoon chopped fresh basil
½ teaspoon Dijon mustard

2 5-ounce packages mixed baby greens
3 pears, halved, cored, thinly sliced
¾ cup pine nuts, toasted

Combine first 8 ingredients in medium bowl; whisk to blend. Season dressing to taste with salt and pepper. (*Can be made 4 hours ahead. Cover; refrigerate.*)

Place greens, pears, and pine nuts in large bowl. Add dressing; toss to coat.

10 SERVINGS

Caesar Coleslaw

  1 cup mayonnaise
  ⅓ cup fresh lemon juice
  9 anchovy fillets, finely chopped
  3 garlic cloves, minced
  1 2¼-pound head of savoy cabbage, halved, cored, very thinly sliced (about 16 cups)
16 green onions, thinly sliced
  ½ cup (packed) freshly grated Parmesan cheese

Whisk first 4 ingredients in small bowl to blend. Season dressing to taste with salt and pepper. Place cabbage and green onions in large bowl. Add dressing and toss to coat. (*Can be prepared 1 day ahead. Cover and refrigerate.*)

Mix cheese into coleslaw. Transfer to large shallow bowl and serve.

8 SERVINGS

Rice Salad with Feta, Citrus, and Mint

  4 cups water
  2 cups uncooked white rice
1½ teaspoons salt

  ½ cup fresh orange juice
  ½ cup olive oil
  ¼ cup fresh lemon juice
  4 teaspoons grated orange peel
  2 teaspoons grated lemon peel
  ½ teaspoon ground cinnamon

30 cherry tomatoes, halved
  7 small pickling cucumbers, diced (about 4 cups)
  1 cup sliced green onions
  ½ cup chopped fresh mint
16 ounces feta cheese, crumbled

Bring 4 cups water, rice, and salt to boil in heavy medium saucepan over high heat, stirring occasionally. Reduce heat to low; cover and cook until rice is tender and water is absorbed, about 20 minutes. Uncover saucepan and cook rice over very low heat until dry, about 5 minutes. Transfer rice to large bowl and cool to room temperature.

Whisk orange juice and next 5 ingredients in small bowl to blend.

Add tomatoes and next 4 ingredients to rice in large bowl. Add dressing; toss. (*Can be made 8 hours ahead; cover and chill. Bring to room temperature and toss before serving.*)

10 SERVINGS

Fruit Salad with Tangerine Dressing

  2 cups ½-inch cubes peeled cored pineapple
  2 cups seedless grapes (preferably a mix of black, red, and green)
  2 cups ½-inch cubes peeled kiwis (about 5 large)
  2 cups cubed peeled seeded tangerines (about 5)
  1 large Fuji apple, quartered, cored, cut into ½-inch cubes
  ¼ cup sugar
  ¼ cup fresh tangerine juice
  ¼ cup slivered fresh mint
  2 tablespoons Grand Marnier or other orange liqueur

Combine all fruit in large bowl. Add sugar, tangerine juice, mint, and liqueur; toss gently to blend. Let stand at least 30 minutes, tossing occasionally. *(Can be made 3 hours ahead. Cover and refrigerate.)*

8 SERVINGS

Fresh mint adds a bright flavor to this refreshing salad, which can be made several hours before guests arrive.

Sicilian Fennel and Orange Salad with Red Onion and Mint

  2 navel oranges or blood oranges
  1 large fennel bulb, halved lengthwise, cored, very thinly sliced crosswise
  ½ cup very thinly sliced red onion
 16 small fresh mint leaves, torn in half
  3 tablespoons extra-virgin olive oil
 20 oil-cured black olives

Cut peel and white pith from oranges. Cut between membranes to release orange segments.

Toss orange segments, fennel, onion, mint, and oil in large bowl to coat. Season salad generously to taste with salt and pepper. Transfer salad to platter. Garnish with olives and serve immediately.

4 SERVINGS

Olive oil blends with the juice from the oranges to create a tangy vinaigrette. Pair the salad with a hearty braised veal or pork dish.

Spinach, Apple, and Cheddar Cheese Salad

¼ cup balsamic vinegar
¼ cup pure maple syrup
¼ cup olive oil

2 6-ounce packages baby spinach leaves
2 large unpeeled Granny Smith apples, halved, cored, thinly sliced
8 ounces extra-sharp cheddar cheese, cut into ½-inch cubes
½ cup chopped toasted walnuts

Combine vinegar, maple syrup, and oil in small bowl; whisk to blend. Season dressing to taste with salt and pepper. *(Can be made 1 day ahead. Cover and chill. Rewhisk before using.)*

Combine spinach, apples, cheese, and walnuts in large bowl. Toss with enough dressing to coat. Season salad to taste with salt and pepper. Transfer salad to serving bowl.

8 SERVINGS

Roasted-Beet and Avocado Salad with Citrus Vinaigrette

4   large beets
2   tablespoons balsamic vinegar
2   teaspoons plus 7 tablespoons olive oil

6   tablespoons fresh orange juice
3   tablespoons fresh lime juice
1   shallot, chopped
¾   teaspoon grated orange peel

15 ounces mixed greens
8   ounces queso fresco cheese, crumbled
4   ripe avocados, halved, pitted, peeled, sliced

The beets can be roasted a day ahead; the rest is quick and easy.

Preheat oven to 400°F. Line rimmed baking sheet with foil. Using vegetable peeler, peel beets. Cut into ½-inch-thick wedges. Place beets on foil in single layer. Sprinkle with vinegar, 2 teaspoons oil, salt, and pepper. Cover tightly with another sheet of foil. Bake until juices form, about 20 minutes. Uncover and bake until juices evaporate and beets are tender, tossing occasionally, about 40 minutes. Cool. (*Can be made 1 day ahead. Cover; chill.*)

Whisk orange juice, lime juice, shallot, and orange peel in medium bowl. Gradually whisk in 7 tablespoons oil. Season dressing with salt and pepper.

Place greens and cheese in bowl. Toss with ½ cup dressing. Mound greens on platter. Surround with beets and avocados. Drizzle remaining dressing over beets and avocados. Sprinkle with salt and pepper.

10 SERVINGS

Mixed Greens with Sautéed Bay Scallops

  2 tablespoons orange juice

1½ tablespoons plus 2 teaspoons balsamic vinegar

 ¼ cup plus 1 tablespoon extra-virgin olive oil

  2 large oranges

  1 teaspoon grated orange peel

  1 teaspoon grated lime peel

  1 teaspoon fresh lime juice

 ¼ teaspoon ground black pepper

  1 pound bay scallops

10 cups (lightly packed) mixed bitter greens (such as escarole, radicchio, endive, and frisée)

16 grape tomatoes, halved

Whisk orange juice and 1½ tablespoons vinegar in medium bowl to blend. Whisk in ¼ cup oil. Season with salt and pepper.

Cut peel and pith from oranges; cut between membranes to release segments.

Whisk 1 tablespoon oil, orange peel, lime peel, lime juice, pepper, and 2 teaspoons vinegar in bowl for marinade. (*Dressing, oranges, and marinade can be made 4 hours ahead; chill. Bring dressing back to room temperature.*) Mix scallops into marinade. Let stand 10 minutes.

Heat large nonstick skillet over high heat. Add scallops with marinade and sauté until just cooked through, about 2 minutes. Season scallops to taste with salt.

Toss orange segments, mixed greens, and tomatoes in large bowl with enough dressing to coat. Divide salad among plates. Place scallops atop salads.

8 SERVINGS

Sweet Potato Salad with Maple Dressing

DRESSING

¼ cup extra-virgin olive oil

2 tablespoons pure maple syrup

2 tablespoons orange juice

2 tablespoons Sherry wine vinegar or balsamic vinegar

1 tablespoon fresh lemon juice

2 teaspoons minced peeled fresh ginger

½ teaspoon ground cinnamon

¼ teaspoon ground nutmeg

SALAD

6 pounds red-skinned sweet potatoes (yams), peeled, cut into
¾-inch cubes

1 cup chopped green onions

1 cup chopped fresh parsley

1 cup pecans, toasted, coarsely chopped

½ cup golden raisins

½ cup brown raisins

FOR DRESSING: Whisk all ingredients to blend in small bowl. Season dressing to taste with salt and pepper.

FOR SALAD: Steam sweet potatoes in batches until potatoes are just tender, about 10 minutes per batch. Transfer sweet potatoes to large bowl. Cool to room temperature. Add green onions, parsley, pecans, and all raisins. Pour dressing over; toss gently to blend. Season salad to taste with salt and pepper. (*Can be made 2 hours ahead. Let stand at room temperature.*)

12 SERVINGS

Open-House Buffet
for 24

Merlot and *Chardonnay*

Herbed Crab Cakes
(*page 11; double recipe*)

**Indian-Spiced Chicken Kebabs
with Cilantro Chutney**
(*page 17*)

Mixed Nuts

Purchased Baked Ham

Herbed Quinoa Pilaf
(*page 144; double recipe*)

**Sweet Potato Salad with
Maple Dressing**
(*at left; double recipe*)

Roasted Vegetables

**Tropical Carrot Cake with
Coconut Cream Cheese Frosting**
(*page 202*)

Turtle Bars
(*page 229*)

Fruit Platter

Coffee and *Tea*

Grilled Corn Salad with Lima Beans and Tomatoes

¾ cup (about) olive oil
2 tablespoons apple cider vinegar
1 large shallot, finely chopped
6 medium ears fresh corn, husked
2 cups frozen baby lima beans
2 bunches watercress, thick stems trimmed, sprigs torn in half
2 cups halved teardrop tomatoes or cherry tomatoes
1 cup coarsely grated Parmesan cheese or crumbled soft fresh goat cheese
1 cup halved pitted Kalamata olives
Roasted Red Pepper and Tomato Sauce (see recipe below)

Prepare barbecue (medium-high heat). Whisk ½ cup oil, vinegar, and shallot in small bowl. Set dressing aside. Brush corn with remaining ¼ cup oil; sprinkle with salt and pepper. Grill until tender and beginning to char in spots, turning often, about 10 minutes. Cool slightly. Cut corn from cobs. Transfer to large bowl. Cook lima beans in boiling salted water until just tender, about 4 minutes. Drain. Rinse with cold water; drain. Mix lima beans into corn. Mix watercress and tomatoes into corn mixture. Add dressing and toss to coat. Season salad with salt and pepper. Sprinkle with cheese; garnish with olives. Serve, passing roasted pepper sauce.

8 SERVINGS

Roasted Red Pepper and Tomato Sauce

1 7- to 8-ounce red bell pepper
2 plum tomatoes
¼ cup extra-virgin olive oil
1 tablespoon apple cider vinegar
1 garlic clove, peeled
⅛ teaspoon cayenne pepper

Char bell pepper and tomatoes directly over gas flame or in broiler until blackened on all sides. Transfer tomatoes to plate. Enclose pepper in paper bag 10 minutes. Peel, halve, and seed tomatoes; place in blender. Peel, seed, and chop pepper; add to blender. Add oil, vinegar, garlic, and cayenne; blend until smooth. Season sauce with salt and pepper. (*Can be made 1 day ahead. Cover and chill.*)

MAKES ABOUT 1 CUP

Leeks Vinaigrette with Smoked Whitefish

- 1 shallot, minced
- 2 tablespoons fresh lemon juice
- 1 tablespoon Champagne vinegar or white wine vinegar
- 1 teaspoon Dijon mustard
- ½ cup olive oil

- 8 whole small (1 inch in diameter) leeks
- 1 Gala apple, cored, cut into ¼-inch cubes
- 8 ounces smoked whitefish, carefully boned, coarsely flaked

Whisk shallot, lemon juice, vinegar, and mustard in small bowl to blend. Gradually whisk in oil. Season vinaigrette with salt and pepper.

Trim root end of leeks, leaving core intact. Remove any tough outer leaves. Cut each leek in half lengthwise. Bring large pot of salted water to boil. Add leeks; reduce heat to low and simmer until leeks are soft, about 12 minutes. Drain. Arrange leeks on platter. Spoon ½ cup vinaigrette over; let stand until leeks cool, about 1 hour. Add apple to remaining vinaigrette. Divide leeks among 8 plates. Spoon fish over leeks. Top fish with apple mixture and serve.

8 SERVINGS

Cheddar and Cream Scones

    2 cups all purpose flour
    1 tablespoon baking powder
    2 teaspoons sugar
    ¼ teaspoon salt
    ½ cup (1 stick) chilled unsalted butter, cut into ½-inch cubes
    1 cup (packed) coarsely grated extra-sharp white cheddar cheese (about 4 ounces)
    ¾ cup chilled whipping cream
    1 large egg

Preheat oven to 375°F. Blend flour, baking powder, sugar, and salt in processor. Using on/off turns, cut in butter until mixture resembles coarse meal. Add cheese and cut in using on/off turns. Whisk cream and egg in small bowl. With machine running, add cream mixture through feed tube. Process just until dough begins to clump together (do not overmix).

Turn dough out onto lightly floured work surface. Gather dough together; divide in half. Pat each half into 6-inch round. Cut each round into 6 wedges. Transfer to ungreased baking sheet, spacing 2 inches apart.

Bake scones until golden and tester inserted into center comes out clean, about 20 minutes. Transfer scones to rack and cool at least 10 minutes. Serve warm or at room temperature. (*Can be made 8 hours ahead. Let stand at room temperature. If desired, rewarm in 350°F oven about 5 minutes.*)

MAKES 12

Onion and Fennel-Seed Biscuits

Post-Hike Lunch for 6

Hominy, Tomato, and
Chile Soup
(page 29)

Baked Honey Ham

Onion and Fennel Seed Biscuits
(at left)

Coleslaw

Lemonade and *Iced Tea*

Brownie Cupcakes with
Peanut Butter Frosting
(page 201)

7 tablespoons chilled unsalted butter
1 cup chopped onion
¾ teaspoon fennel seeds, lightly crushed

2 cups all purpose flour
2 tablespoons sugar
2½ teaspoons baking powder
1 teaspoon salt
¾ cup (or more) chilled whole milk

Preheat oven to 400°F. Line large baking sheet with parchment paper. Melt 2 tablespoons butter in small skillet over medium heat. Add onion and fennel seeds. Cover and cook until onion begins to brown, stirring occasionally, about 7 minutes. Cool completely.

Whisk flour, sugar, baking powder, and salt in large bowl to blend. Cut remaining 5 tablespoons butter into ½-inch cubes; add to flour mixture. Rub in with fingertips until coarse meal forms. Add ¾ cup milk, tossing with fork. Mix in additional milk by tablespoonfuls if mixture is dry. Gently stir in onion mixture. Turn dough out onto floured surface; pat out to ½-inch thickness. Using 2-inch-round cutter, cut out dough rounds. Gather scraps, pat dough out, and cut out more rounds. Arrange rounds 1 inch apart on prepared sheet.

Bake biscuits until cooked through and golden on top, about 15 minutes. Serve biscuits warm.

MAKES 18

Golden Brioche

⅓ cup warm water (105°F to 115°F)

⅓ cup warm milk (105°F to 115°F)

2 envelopes dry yeast

3¾ cups all purpose flour

2 teaspoons salt

3 large eggs

¼ cup sugar

1½ cups (3 sticks) unsalted butter, each stick cut into 4 pieces, room temperature

1 egg, beaten to blend with 1 tablespoon water (for glaze)

Place ⅓ cup warm water, warm milk, and yeast in bowl of standing heavy-duty mixer; stir until yeast dissolves. Fit mixer with dough hook. Add flour and salt to bowl; mix on low speed just until flour is moistened, about 10 seconds. Scrape sides and bottom of bowl. Beat in 3 eggs on low speed, then add sugar. Increase speed to medium and beat until dough comes together, about 3 minutes. Reduce speed to low. Add butter, 1 piece at a time, beating until each piece is almost incorporated before adding next (dough will be soft and batter-like). Increase speed to medium-high and beat until dough pulls away from sides of bowl, about 7 minutes.

Cover bowl with plastic wrap. Let dough rise at room temperature until almost doubled in volume, about 1 hour. Lift up dough around edges and allow dough to fall and deflate in bowl. Cover bowl with plastic and chill until dough stops rising, lifting up dough around edges and allowing dough to fall and deflate in bowl every 30 minutes, about 2 hours total. Cover bowl with plastic; chill dough overnight.

Butter and flour three 7½x3½x2-inch loaf pans. Divide dough into 3 equal pieces. Cut each dough piece into 4 equal pieces. Roll each into 3½-inch-long log, forming 12 logs total. Arrange 4 logs crosswise in bottom of each prepared loaf pan. Place loaf pans on baking sheet. Cover pans with waxed paper. Let loaves rise at room temperature until dough almost fills pans, about 2 hours.

Preheat oven to 400°F. Gently brush top of loaves with egg glaze. Bake until loaves are golden brown and sound hollow when tapped, about 30 minutes. Cool in pans on racks 15 minutes. Turn loaves out onto racks; cool at least 1 hour. *(Can be made ahead. Cool completely. Wrap loaves in foil; place in resealable plastic bags and store at room temperature 1 day or freeze up to 1 month. Rewarm room-temperature or thawed loaves wrapped in foil in 350°F oven about 15 minutes, if desired.)*

MAKES 3 LOAVES

The big bowl and tireless motor of a standing mixer take the heavy work out of preparing these tender brioche loaves.

Jalapeño Corn Muffins

Room-temperature butter
1 cup all purpose flour
1 cup yellow cornmeal
¼ cup sugar
1 tablespoon baking powder
1 teaspoon salt
4 large eggs
¾ cup whole milk
¼ cup corn oil
2 tablespoons minced seeded jalapeño chiles
2 cups fresh corn kernels or frozen, thawed (about 9 ounces)

Preheat oven to 375°F. Butter 12-cup muffin pan. Whisk flour, cornmeal, sugar, baking powder, and salt in medium bowl. Whisk eggs, milk, corn oil, and jalapeños in large bowl. Add dry ingredients to egg mixture, stirring until evenly moistened (do not overmix). Fold in corn kernels.

Divide batter among muffin cups. Bake until golden and tester inserted into center comes out clean, about 25 minutes. Turn out of pan. Serve warm or at room temperature, preferably within 6 hours.

MAKES 12

Potato and Olive Focaccia

1¼ pounds russet potatoes, peeled, cut into ½-inch cubes
2 cups water

½ cup lukewarm (105°F to 115°F) whole milk
1 ¼-ounce envelope active dry yeast
1 teaspoon sugar
4 cups (or more) unbleached all purpose flour
1 tablespoon salt
½ teaspoon ground black pepper

Nonstick olive oil spray
Olive oil
10 ounces large Kalamata olives, pitted, quartered (about 2 cups)

Combine potatoes and 2 cups water in medium saucepan. Bring to boil over high heat. Reduce heat to medium, partially cover, and simmer until potatoes are tender, about 15 minutes. Drain, reserving ½ cup cooking water. Place potatoes in large bowl and mash well; cool 10 minutes.

Mix ½ cup cooking water and milk in small bowl. Cool to 105°F to 115°F if necessary. Sprinkle yeast and sugar over; stir to dissolve. Let stand until yeast mixture bubbles, about 8 minutes. Using flexible spatula, stir yeast mixture into potatoes. Mix in 1 cup flour, salt, and pepper. Mix in 3 cups flour, 1 cup at a time. Knead dough in bowl until smooth, sprinkling lightly with flour if sticky, about 4 minutes. Cover bowl with plastic. Let dough rise in warm draft-free area until doubled in volume, about 50 minutes. (*Can be made 1 day ahead. Flatten dough in bowl. Cover; chill. Let stand at room temperature 1 hour before continuing.*)

Spray 2 heavy large baking sheets with nonstick spray, then brush each with olive oil. Divide dough in half. Place dough on floured surface. Flatten each to ½-inch thickness; sprinkle each with half of olives. Roll up dough to enclose olives and knead to distribute olives evenly, about 2 minutes. Place each piece of dough on 1 prepared sheet. Press and stretch each out to 14x10-inch rectangle. Using small sharp knife, make ten 4-inch-long cuts in each, parallel to short side and cutting through to baking sheet. Gently pull cuts open, making coarse web pattern. Brush dough with oil. Cover each loosely with plastic. Let rise until dough is slightly puffed (cuts will narrow), about 30 minutes.

Position 1 rack in top third of oven and 1 rack in bottom third; preheat to 425°F. Bake breads 15 minutes. Reverse sheets; bake until golden brown, about 15 minutes longer. Transfer breads to racks; cool. (*Can be made 4 hours ahead. Let stand at room temperature.*)

MAKES 2 LOAVES

Molasses-Glazed Pecan Scones

2 cups all purpose flour

¾ cup (packed) golden brown sugar

1 teaspoon baking powder

½ teaspoon baking soda

½ teaspoon salt

10 tablespoons (1¼ sticks) chilled unsalted butter, cut into
½-inch cubes

¾ cup pecans, toasted, broken into pieces

⅔ cup buttermilk

2 large egg yolks

1 teaspoon maple extract

2 tablespoons whipping cream

⅔ cup powdered sugar

½ teaspoon mild-flavored (light) molasses

These oversize wedge-shaped scones have a lovely maple flavor and a light muffin-like texture.

Position rack in center of oven and preheat to 400°F. Combine flour, ¼ cup brown sugar, baking powder, baking soda, and salt in large bowl; whisk to blend. Add 6 tablespoons butter; using fingertips, rub in until butter is reduced to pea-size pieces. Mix in pecans. Whisk buttermilk, egg yolks, and extract in medium bowl; add to flour mixture. Toss with fork until dough comes together in moist clumps. Gather dough into ball. Press dough out on lightly floured surface to 8-inch round; cut into 6 wedges.

Arrange wedges 1 inch apart on ungreased baking sheet. Bake until tester inserted into center comes out clean, about 16 minutes; transfer to rack.

Whisk ½ cup brown sugar, 4 tablespoons butter, and cream in heavy small saucepan over low heat until sugar dissolves. Remove pan from heat. Whisk in powdered sugar and molasses. Spread glaze over warm scones. Let stand until glaze sets, at least 30 minutes.

MAKES 6

Spiced Pumpkin Bread with Dried Cranberries

    2 cups all purpose flour
    2 teaspoons pumpkin pie spice
    1 teaspoon baking powder
   ¾ teaspoon salt
   ½ teaspoon baking soda
    6 tablespoons (¾ stick) unsalted butter, room temperature
    1 cup plus 1 tablespoon sugar
    2 large eggs
    1 cup canned pure pumpkin
    1 teaspoon vanilla extract
   ⅔ cup buttermilk
   ½ cup dried sweetened cranberries
   ½ cup coarsely chopped walnuts

Preheat oven to 350°F. Butter 9¼x5¼x3-inch loaf pan. Line bottom and 2 long sides with waxed paper. Whisk first 5 ingredients in medium bowl to blend. Using electric mixer, beat butter in large bowl until fluffy. Gradually add 1 cup sugar. Beat in eggs, 1 at a time. Beat in pumpkin, then vanilla. Beat in dry ingredients alternately with buttermilk in 2 additions each. Fold in cranberries and nuts. Transfer batter to pan. Sprinkle with 1 tablespoon sugar.

Bake bread until tester inserted into center comes out clean, about 1 hour 10 minutes. Cool in pan on rack 15 minutes. Cut around bread at short ends to loosen. Turn out onto rack; peel off paper. Cool. (*Can be made 2 days ahead. Wrap and store at room temperature.*)

MAKES 1 LOAF

Walnut and Rosemary Loaf

   2¼ cups very warm whole milk (120°F)
     3 tablespoons sugar
     2 tablespoons (¼ stick) unsalted butter, cut into ½-inch pieces, room temperature
     2 teaspoons salt
    ¼ cup warm water (110°F to 115°F)
     2 envelopes active dry yeast

     1 large egg, beaten to blend
   6½ cups (about) all purpose flour

     1 cup coarsely chopped walnuts
     2 teaspoons chopped fresh rosemary
        Vegetable oil

     1 large egg yolk, beaten with 1 tablespoon whole milk (for glaze)

Pour milk into large bowl. Mix in sugar, butter, and salt; cool to luke-warm. Place ¼ cup warm water in small bowl; mix in yeast. Let yeast mixture stand 6 minutes.

Stir yeast mixture and 1 egg into milk mixture. Mix in 4 cups flour. Beat with wooden spoon until smooth. Cover bowl with plastic; let sponge stand until bubbles appear at edge, about 15 minutes.

Mix nuts and rosemary into sponge. Mix in flour, ⅓ cupful at a time, until soft, slightly sticky dough forms. Turn dough out onto floured surface and knead until smooth and no longer sticky, sprin-kling with flour as needed, about 10 minutes. Brush clean large bowl with oil. Add dough; turn to coat. Cover bowl with plastic. Let dough rise in warm draft-free area until doubled in volume, about 1 hour.

Brush two 8½ x 4½ x 2½-inch nonstick loaf pans with oil. Punch dough down and turn out onto work surface; shape into two 8-inch-long loaves. Place in pans. Let rise, uncovered, until almost doubled in volume, about 45 minutes.

Position rack in bottom third of oven and preheat to 375°F. Using serrated knife, make shallow cut down center of each loaf. Brush loaves with glaze. Bake until golden and crusty, about 35 minutes. Turn breads out of pans. Cool on racks.

MAKES 2 LOAVES

Tropical Carrot Cake with
Coconut Cream Cheese Frosting
(page 202)

Desserts

Apple Crostata with Crystallized Ginger

CRUST

1½ cups all purpose flour
1½ tablespoons sugar
½   teaspoon (scant) salt
10 tablespoons (1¼ sticks) chilled unsalted butter,
      cut into ½-inch cubes
3   tablespoons (or more) ice water

FILLING

1½ pounds medium-size Golden Delicious apples,
      peeled, halved, cored, cut into ⅛-inch-thick
      slices (about 5½ cups)
5   tablespoons sugar
2   tablespoons (packed) minced crystallized ginger
2   teaspoons fresh lemon juice

2   tablespoons (¼ stick) unsalted butter, cut into ½-inch cubes
2   tablespoons (about) whole milk

⅓   cup apricot preserves, warmed
      Vanilla ice cream or sweetened whipped cream

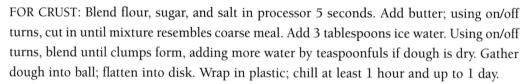

FOR CRUST: Blend flour, sugar, and salt in processor 5 seconds. Add butter; using on/off turns, cut in until mixture resembles coarse meal. Add 3 tablespoons ice water. Using on/off turns, blend until clumps form, adding more water by teaspoonfuls if dough is dry. Gather dough into ball; flatten into disk. Wrap in plastic; chill at least 1 hour and up to 1 day.

FOR FILLING: Position rack in center of oven and preheat to 425°F. Combine apples, 3 tablespoons sugar, crystallized ginger, and lemon juice in large bowl; toss gently to blend.

Roll out dough on large sheet of parchment paper to 14-inch round. Transfer parchment with dough to large baking sheet. Arrange ¾ of apple mixture in center of dough, mounding just slightly, forming 8-inch-diameter circle and leaving 3-inch plain border. Overlap remaining apple slices in concentric circles atop apple layer. Fold plain edge of crust over apples, leaving apples exposed in center. Gently fold and pinch dough edge to seal any cracks. Sprinkle apples with 1 tablespoon sugar, then dot apples with butter. Brush crust with milk and sprinkle with remaining 1 tablespoon sugar.

Bake crostata until crust is golden brown and apples are tender, about 40 minutes. Remove from oven. Brush apples with warm apricot preserves. Cool on baking sheet 15 minutes. Slide long knife under crostata to loosen. (*Can be made 4 hours ahead. Let stand on sheet at room temperature. Rewarm in 425°F oven 5 minutes before serving.*) Serve warm with vanilla ice cream or sweetened whipped cream, as desired.

8 SERVINGS

Strawberry Ice Box Pie with Almond Crust

CRUST

1	cup slivered almonds, toasted
½	cup graham cracker crumbs
¼	cup sugar
6	tablespoons (¾ stick) unsalted butter, melted

FILLING

5	cups quartered hulled strawberries (about 24 ounces)
1	cup sugar
¼	cup cornstarch
2	tablespoons fresh lemon juice
2	teaspoons grated orange peel

1½ cups chilled whipping cream

An easy press-in crust of ground graham crackers and toasted almonds is topped with a fresh strawberry filling and whipped cream. Chill the pie at least two hours before serving.

FOR CRUST: Position rack in center of oven; preheat to 350°F. Butter 9-inch-diameter glass pie dish. Coarsely chop almonds in processor. Add graham cracker crumbs and sugar; process until finely ground. Add butter; process until evenly moistened. Press crumb mixture onto bottom and up sides of prepared pie dish.

Bake crust until set, about 12 minutes. Cool completely on rack.

FOR FILLING: Place 2 cups strawberries in medium saucepan. Mash strawberries with potato masher until chunky. Add sugar, cornstarch, and lemon juice. Stir over medium-high heat until sugar dissolves and mixture boils and thickens, about 3 minutes. Transfer to bowl. Cool to room temperature. Stir in 3 cups strawberries and grated orange peel. Mound filling in crust. Chill pie until cold and set, at least 2 hours and up to 6 hours.

Using electric mixer, beat cream in large bowl until peaks form. Spread whipped cream decoratively over filling. Cut pie into wedges and serve.

6 SERVINGS

Plum Streusel Pie

CRUST

1¼ cups all purpose flour

½ teaspoon sugar

½ teaspoon grated lemon peel

¼ teaspoon salt

½ cup (1 stick) chilled unsalted butter, cut into ½-inch cubes

1 large egg yolk beaten to blend with 3 tablespoons cold water

FILLING AND TOPPING

¾ cup finely chopped walnuts (about 3 ounces)

½ cup all purpose flour

3 tablespoons (packed) golden brown sugar

1½ teaspoons ground cinnamon

3 tablespoons chilled unsalted butter, cut into ½-inch cubes

¾ cup sugar

¼ cup cornstarch

½ teaspoon ground nutmeg

1½ pounds plums (about 5 large), halved, pitted, cut into ½-inch-thick wedges

1 large egg beaten with 2 teaspoons water (for glaze)

Vanilla ice cream

FOR CRUST: Blend flour, sugar, lemon peel, and salt in processor. Add butter; using on/off turns, cut in until pea-size pieces form. With machine running, pour egg mixture through feed tube and blend just until dough forms ball. Gather dough into disk; wrap tightly in plastic wrap and refrigerate at least 2 hours. (*Can be made up to 3 days ahead. Keep chilled.*)

Roll out dough between 2 lightly floured sheets of waxed paper to ¼-inch thickness. Peel off top sheet of paper. Invert crust into 9-inch glass pie dish; peel off paper. Fold edges under to form rim; crimp edges. Refrigerate 1 hour.

FOR FILLING AND TOPPING: Preheat oven to 400°F. Mix walnuts, flour, brown sugar, and ½ teaspoon cinnamon in medium bowl to blend. Add butter and rub in with fingertips until coarse meal forms. Set streusel aside. Whisk ¾ cup sugar, cornstarch, nutmeg, and remaining 1 teaspoon cinnamon in large bowl. Add plums and toss to coat.

Place pie dish on baking sheet. Brush inside of pie shell lightly with egg glaze. Transfer plum filling to pie shell, mounding slightly in center. Sprinkle streusel topping evenly over filling. Bake pie 15 minutes; reduce oven temperature to 375°F. Bake until filling bubbles at edges, about 35 minutes, covering crust edges with foil during last 15 minutes if browning too quickly. Cool pie on rack. (*Can be made 8 hours ahead. Cover and let stand at room temperature.*) Cut pie into wedges. Serve with ice cream.

8 SERVINGS

Fresh Blueberry Tart

CRUST

1¼ cups all purpose flour

3 tablespoons (packed) powdered sugar

¼ teaspoon salt

10 tablespoons (1¼ sticks) chilled unsalted butter, cut into ½-inch cubes

FILLING

¾ cup sugar

3 tablespoons cornstarch

Pinch of salt

2 tablespoons cold water

2 tablespoons fresh lemon juice

1 tablespoon unsalted butter

1 teaspoon grated lemon peel

6 cups fresh blueberries (from about seven ½-pint containers)

Lightly sweetened whipped cream

FOR CRUST: Preheat oven to 350°F. Blend flour, sugar, and salt in processor 5 seconds. Add butter; using on/off turns, blend until clumps form. Gather dough into ball. Press dough over bottom and up sides of 10-inch-diameter tart pan with removable bottom; pierce all over with fork. Bake crust until golden, about 25 minutes. Cool completely.

FOR FILLING: Whisk sugar, cornstarch, and salt in medium saucepan to blend. Gradually add 2 tablespoons cold water and lemon juice, whisking until smooth. Add butter and lemon peel. Add 2 cups berries and mash coarsely with potato masher. Cook over medium heat until mixture thickens and boils, stirring occasionally. Remove from heat. Fold in 4 cups berries. Transfer to crust. Chill until cold, at least 1 hour. *(Can be made 1 day ahead. Cover loosely with foil and keep chilled.)*

Remove tart from pan. Cut into wedges; serve with whipped cream.

8 SERVINGS

This stunning dessert is speedy since the filling is cooked on the stove, not baked.

Walnut Frangipane and Banana Tartlets

2/3 cup walnuts, toasted, cooled

1/3 cup all purpose flour

1/4 teaspoon baking powder

1/8 teaspoon salt

1/2 cup (1 stick) unsalted butter, room temperature

5 tablespoons plus 8 teaspoons sugar

1/4 cup plus 1 teaspoon (packed) golden brown sugar

2 large eggs

1 17.3-ounce package frozen puff pastry (2 sheets), thawed

3 small bananas, cut on diagonal into 3x1/3-inch ovals

1/4 cup apricot jam, heated

Powdered sugar

Blend first 4 ingredients in processor until nuts are finely ground. Using electric mixer, beat butter, 5 tablespoons sugar, and brown sugar in bowl until blended. Beat in eggs, then ground walnut mixture. *(Can be made 1 day ahead. Cover and chill.)*

Roll out each pastry sheet on lightly floured surface to 10-inch square. Using 5-inch-diameter plate as guide, cut out 4 rounds from each square. Using tip of small knife, score 4-inch-diameter circle in center of each 5-inch round (do not cut completely through pastry). Pierce 4-inch centers thoroughly with fork. Place pastry rounds on large baking sheet. Chill until very cold, at least 1 hour and up to 1 day.

Preheat oven to 375°F. Spread 2½ tablespoons frangipane over 4-inch center of each pastry (reserve remaining frangipane for another use). Arrange bananas on frangipane. Sprinkle bananas on each tart with 1 teaspoon sugar. Bake until pastry is deep golden, about 25 minutes.

Brush bananas with warm jam. Sift powdered sugar over tartlets.

Frangipane is typically a ground almond filling; here, walnuts are used in a similar preparation. You can make the frangipane and cut out the pastry one day ahead.

8 SERVINGS

Triple-Chocolate Pudding Pie with Cappuccino Cream

CRUST

- 9 whole chocolate graham crackers
- 1 tablespoon sugar
- Pinch of salt
- 6 tablespoons unsalted butter, melted

FILLING

- 1¼ cups sugar
- ½ cup unsweetened cocoa powder
- ¼ cup cornstarch
- 3½ cups half and half
- 4 large egg yolks
- 3½ ounces bittersweet (not unsweetened) or semisweet chocolate, chopped
- 3 ounces unsweetened chocolate, chopped
- 2 tablespoons unsalted butter
- 1 teaspoon vanilla extract

TOPPING

- 1 cup chilled whipping cream
- 2 tablespoons powdered sugar
- 1½ teaspoons instant espresso powder
- ½ teaspoon vanilla extract

Chocolate-covered espresso beans

FOR CRUST: Preheat oven to 350°F. Finely grind graham crackers, sugar, and salt in processor. Add butter and blend to moisten crumbs. Firmly press mixture into 9-inch-diameter glass pie dish. Bake until crust sets, about 8 minutes. Cool.

FOR FILLING: Whisk sugar, cocoa, and cornstarch in heavy medium saucepan. Gradually whisk in 1 cup half and half. Whisk in remaining 2½ cups half and half and yolks. Whisk over medium-high heat until mixture thickens and boils, whisking constantly, about 12 minutes. Remove from heat. Add both chocolates and butter; whisk until melted and smooth. Mix in vanilla. Transfer filling to crust. Press plastic wrap directly onto surface of filling and chill until filling sets, at least 6 hours. *(Can be made 2 days ahead. Keep chilled.)*

FOR TOPPING: Beat all ingredients in large bowl until peaks form. *(Can be made 1 day ahead. Cover and refrigerate. Rewhisk to thicken before serving, if necessary.)*

Peel plastic off pie. Cut pie into wedges. Spoon dollop of cream atop each slice. Garnish with chocolate-covered espresso beans and serve.

8 SERVINGS

Caramel-Nut Pie with Dried Cherries

CRUST

1½ cups all purpose flour

½ teaspoon salt

¼ teaspoon baking powder

5 tablespoons chilled unsalted butter, cut into ½-inch cubes

4 tablespoons (or more) ice water

FILLING

1¼ cups dried tart cherries, chopped

½ cup ruby Port

⅔ cup (packed) golden brown sugar

⅔ cup light corn syrup

3 large eggs

¼ cup (½ stick) butter, melted, room temperature

1½ teaspoons vanilla extract

1 cup walnuts, toasted, chopped

Whipped cream

FOR CRUST: Blend flour, salt, and baking powder in processor. Using on/off turns, cut in butter until mixture resembles coarse meal. Add 4 tablespoons ice water. Process just until moist clumps form, adding more water by teaspoonfuls if dough is dry. Form dough into disk. Wrap in plastic; chill until dough is firm enough to roll out, about 30 minutes.

FOR FILLING: Preheat oven to 350°F. Boil cherries and Port in heavy small saucepan until Port is absorbed, stirring often, about 10 minutes. Cool completely.

Using electric mixer, beat brown sugar, corn syrup, eggs, and melted butter in large bowl until foamy. Beat in vanilla. Stir in walnuts and Port-infused cherries.

Roll out dough on floured work surface to 11-inch round; transfer to 9-inch-diameter glass pie dish. Fold overhang under; crimp edges. Pour filling into crust.

Bake pie until crust is golden and filling is brown and just set in center, about 50 minutes. Cool pie completely in dish on rack. Serve with whipped cream.

8 TO 10 SERVINGS

Pear Tarte Tatin with Vanilla and Ginger

1 sheet frozen puff pastry (half of 17.3-ounce package), thawed

½ cup sugar

¼ cup water

1 teaspoon light corn syrup

2 tablespoons (¼ stick) unsalted butter

½ vanilla bean, split lengthwise, seeds scraped into small bowl

1 tablespoon grated peeled fresh ginger

5 medium-size firm Anjou pears (about 2¼ pounds), peeled, halved, cored, each half cut into 4 wedges

Whipped cream

Roll out pastry on lightly floured surface to 10-inch square. Trim edges, making 10-inch-diameter round; pierce round all over with fork. Slide onto rimless baking sheet. Cover and chill pastry while preparing pears or up to 1 day.

Fill large skillet with ice and water; set aside. Stir sugar, ¼ cup water, and corn syrup in heavy 10-inch-diameter nonstick ovenproof skillet over low heat until sugar dissolves. Increase heat and boil until syrup is dark amber color, occasionally swirling and brushing down sides of skillet with wet pastry brush, about 5 minutes. Remove from heat; whisk in butter, then vanilla-bean seeds and ginger (caramel will bubble up). Arrange pears, cut side down and overlapping, in circle in skillet, placing a few around edge, if necessary. Place skillet over medium heat. Cook until pears are tender and syrup thickens enough to coat spoon, about 23 minutes. Place hot skillet atop ice in large skillet to cool pear mixture quickly. *(Can be made 4 hours ahead. Let stand at room temperature.)*

Preheat oven to 375°F. Place puff pastry round atop pear mixture in skillet; tuck in edges around pears. Bake tart until pastry is puffed and golden, about 35 minutes. Cool tart completely in pan at least 1 hour and up to 6 hours.

Preheat oven to 375°F. Rewarm tart in oven 8 minutes. Place platter atop skillet. Using oven mitts, hold skillet and platter together and turn over, releasing tart. Serve tart with whipped cream.

6 TO 8 SERVINGS

Sunday Family Supper for 6

Cannellini Soup with Parmesan Cheese
(page 26)

Roast Chicken with Herbed Olivada
(page 74)

Roasted Potatoes

Escarole Salad

Pinot Gris

Pear Tarte Tartin with Vanilla and Ginger
(at left)

Marsala and Dried-Fig Crostata

FILLING

1¼ pounds dried Calimyrna figs, stemmed, coarsely
    chopped

1¾ cups dry Marsala

1¾ cups water

¼ cup (packed) golden brown sugar

2 cinnamon sticks

⅛ teaspoon ground cloves

CRUST

2¼ cups all purpose flour

½ cup sugar

2 teaspoons fennel seeds

¼ teaspoon salt

½ cup plus 6 tablespoons (1¾ sticks) unsalted butter, room temperature

2 large eggs

Vanilla ice cream

FOR FILLING: Combine all ingredients in heavy large saucepan and bring to boil over high heat. Reduce heat to medium-low. Cover; simmer until figs are very tender, about 1 hour. Uncover; simmer until liquid reduces slightly, about 8 minutes. Transfer to medium bowl. Cool slightly. Refrigerate until cool, stirring occasionally (mixture will be thick), about 45 minutes. Discard cinnamon sticks. (*Can be made 1 day ahead. Cover and keep chilled.*)

FOR CRUST: Preheat oven to 375°F. Mix flour, sugar, fennel seeds, and salt in processor. Add butter and 1 egg. Using on/off turns, process until dough forms. Gather dough into ball; divide in half. Flatten each half into disk. Wrap 1 disk in plastic wrap; refrigerate until cold, at least 30 minutes and up to 1 day. Press remaining dough disk onto bottom and up sides of 10-inch-diameter tart pan with removable bottom. Pierce bottom all over with fork. Chill until firm, about 10 minutes. (*Can be prepared 1 day ahead. Cover and keep chilled.*)

Roll out chilled dough disk on waxed paper to 12-inch round. Transfer to rimless baking sheet. Cut into twelve ¾-inch-wide strips. Chill strips while filling tart. Spread filling in crust. Place 6 dough strips atop filling, spacing evenly. Place remaining 6 strips diagonally atop first 6 strips, forming diamond lattice pattern. Press ends of strips against edge of tart pan to trim. Whisk remaining egg in small bowl to blend; brush over lattice.

Bake tart until juices bubble thickly around edges and crust is deep golden, about 55 minutes. Cool on rack 1 hour. Using small knife, gently loosen tart from pan sides. Remove sides. Serve slightly warm or at room temperature with ice cream.

8 SERVINGS

Raspberry-Chocolate Tart

CRUST

1½ cups chocolate wafer cookie crumbs (about 6 ounces plain chocolate wafers)

6 tablespoons (¾ stick) unsalted butter, melted

¼ cup sugar

FILLING

1 ½-pint container fresh raspberries

½ cup sugar

2 tablespoons water

1 teaspoon fresh lemon juice

1 8-ounce container mascarpone cheese*

½ cup chilled heavy whipping cream

¼ teaspoon vanilla extract

TOPPING

2 ½-pint containers fresh raspberries

⅓ cup seedless raspberry preserves

This dessert has a baked chocolate-cookie crust and a chilled light-and-fluffy filling of pureed fresh raspberries folded into whipped mascarpone cheese.

FOR CRUST: Preheat oven to 350°F. Combine cookie crumbs, melted butter, and sugar in processor; process until crumbs are evenly moistened. Press mixture onto bottom and up sides of 9-inch-diameter tart pan with removable bottom. Bake crust until set, about 10 minutes. Cool crust completely on rack.

FOR FILLING: Combine raspberries, ¼ cup sugar, 2 tablespoons water, and lemon juice in processor. Puree until smooth. Pour puree through strainer set over medium bowl, pressing on solids to extract as much liquid as possible; discard seeds in strainer. Combine mascarpone, heavy whipping cream, vanilla, and remaining ¼ cup sugar in another medium bowl. Using electric mixer, beat until mixture is smooth and stiff peaks form. Fold in raspberry puree. Spread filling evenly in cooled chocolate crust. Cover and refrigerate tart overnight.

FOR TOPPING: Arrange fresh raspberries in concentric circles atop tart. Stir raspberry preserves in heavy small saucepan over medium-low heat until melted to form glaze. Brush glaze over fresh raspberries. Refrigerate tart at least 1 hour and up to 4 hours.

Remove tart pan sides. Place tart on platter and serve.

Italian cream cheese, available at Italian markets and many supermarkets.

8 SERVINGS

Cherry Pie with Orange and Cinnamon

CRUST

⅓ cup whole milk

1 tablespoon distilled white vinegar

2 cups all purpose flour

½ teaspoon salt

1 cup chilled solid vegetable shortening, cut into ½-inch cubes

FILLING

⅔ cup plus ¼ cup sugar

3 tablespoons cornstarch

2 tablespoons orange juice

1 tablespoon grated orange peel

1 teaspoon ground cinnamon

¼ teaspoon almond extract

⅛ teaspoon salt

5 cups pitted fresh cherries (about 2½ pounds) or frozen pitted sweet dark cherries, thawed, drained (about 26 ounces frozen)

1 egg, beaten to blend with 2 teaspoons water (for glaze)

FOR CRUST: Whisk milk and vinegar in small bowl to blend. Whisk flour and salt in medium bowl to blend; add shortening and rub in with fingertips until mixture resembles coarse meal. Stir in milk mixture; briefly knead in bowl just until dough comes together. Gather dough into ball. Divide into 2 pieces, 1 slightly larger than the other. Flatten each into disk. Wrap separately in plastic; chill 30 minutes.

FOR FILLING: Mix ⅔ cup sugar and next 6 ingredients in large bowl to combine. Add cherries; toss to blend. Let stand 30 minutes.

Preheat oven to 400°F. Roll out larger dough disk on lightly floured work surface to 13-inch round (crust will be thin). Transfer to 10-inch-diameter glass pie dish. Roll out second disk on lightly floured work surface to 12x8-inch rectangle. Using fluted pastry wheel or sharp knife, cut rectangle lengthwise into nine ¾-inch-wide strips. Spoon cherry filling into crust. Place 5 dough strips across pie in 1 direction and 4 in opposite direction, forming lattice. Press strip ends and edge of crust together to seal. Crimp edges decoratively. Brush lattice and edges with egg glaze. Sprinkle ¼ cup sugar over lattice.

Bake pie 20 minutes. Cover crust edges with foil collar to prevent overbrowning. Continue to bake until filling bubbles and crust is golden, about 40 minutes longer. Transfer to rack; cool at least 1 hour.

8 SERVINGS

Steak on the Grill for 8

Crudités with Ranch Dip

Barbecued Cowboy Steaks
(page 48)

Heirloom Tomato Salad with Blue Cheese
(page 152)

Grilled Asparagus

Cabernet Sauvignon

Cherry Pie with Orange and Cinnamon
(at left)

Apple Crumble with Vanilla Ice Cream

2½   cups old-fashioned oats
1½   cups (packed) golden brown sugar
  1   cup all purpose flour
  1   cup (2 sticks) chilled unsalted butter, cut into ½-inch cubes

     Nonstick vegetable oil spray
  4   pounds large Granny Smith apples, peeled, halved, cored, each half cut into 6 slices
  3   tablespoons fresh lemon juice
  1   tablespoon ground cinnamon

     Vanilla ice cream

Mix oats, 1 cup sugar, and flour in bowl. Add butter; rub in with fingertips until topping comes together in moist clumps. (*Can be made 1 day ahead. Cover; chill.*)

Preheat oven to 375°F. Spray 13x9x2-inch glass baking dish with nonstick spray. Mix sliced apples, lemon juice, ground cinnamon, and remaining ½ cup brown sugar in bowl. Transfer to dish. Sprinkle topping over.

Bake crumble until apples are tender and topping is brown and crisp, about 55 minutes. Cool slightly. Spoon warm crumble into bowls. Serve with ice cream.

10 TO 12 SERVINGS

Cherry-Berry Crisp

TOPPING

- 1 cup all purpose flour
- ½ cup (packed) golden brown sugar
- ½ cup old-fashioned oats
- ½ teaspoon ground cinnamon
- 10 tablespoons chilled unsalted butter, cut into ½-inch cubes

FRUIT

- 3½ pounds cherries, stemmed, pitted
- 1½ cups sugar
- 3 tablespoons quick-cooking tapioca
- 2 tablespoons fresh lemon juice
- 1 teaspoon almond extract
- 3 ½-pint baskets raspberries

Vanilla ice cream

Buy a cherry pitter at a cookware store, or stem the cherries and use a chopstick to push the pits out through the other end.

FOR TOPPING: Mix flour, brown sugar, oats, and cinnamon in medium bowl. Add butter and rub in with fingertips until mixture comes together in moist clumps. (*Can be made 1 day ahead. Cover; chill.*)

FOR FRUIT: Preheat oven to 375°F. Mix cherries, sugar, tapioca, lemon juice, and almond extract in heavy large pot. Bring to boil over medium-high heat, stirring often; let cool 10 minutes. Transfer mixture to 13x9x2-inch glass baking dish. Sprinkle raspberries over. Sprinkle topping evenly over berries.

Bake crisp until fruit filling bubbles thickly and topping is deep brown, about 40 minutes. Cool 30 minutes. Serve warm with ice cream.

10 SERVINGS

Oranges and Pineapple with Orange-Flower Water and Mint

5 oranges, peel and white pith cut away, fruit cubed (about 2 cups)
½ pineapple, peeled, cored, cut into 1-inch cubes (about 2 cups)
⅓ cup chopped fresh mint leaves
3 tablespoons sugar
2 teaspoons orange-flower water*
1 cinnamon stick, broken in half
4 whole cloves

1 quart fruit sorbet (such as lemon, pineapple, or strawberry)
Fresh mint sprigs

Combine oranges and next 6 ingredients in large bowl; toss to combine. Cover and chill at least 1 hour and up to 6 hours.

Spoon fruit and syrup into bowls. Top each with scoop of sorbet and mint sprigs and serve.

*A flavoring extract available at liquor stores and in the liquor or specialty foods section of supermarkets.

6 SERVINGS

Peaches in Brown Sugar and Rum Sauce with Ice Cream

¼ cup (½ stick) unsalted butter
6 tablespoons (packed) golden brown sugar
¾ teaspoon ground cinnamon
6 ripe peaches, peeled, halved, pitted, each cut into 8 wedges
2 teaspoons vanilla extract
2 tablespoons dark rum
Vanilla or peach ice cream

Melt butter in heavy large skillet over medium heat. Add sugar and cinnamon and cook, stirring often, until sugar begins to dissolve (mixture may clump together). Add peaches and vanilla. Sauté until peaches are tender, stirring occasionally, about 4 minutes. Remove skillet from heat. Stir in rum. Return skillet to heat and cook until sauce thickens, stirring frequently, about 2 minutes. Spoon peaches and sauce over ice cream.

6 SERVINGS

Dinner with the Neighbors for 6

Tomato Bruschetta

Prosciutto-Stuffed Pork Tenderloin with Mushroom Sauce
(page 65)

Green Beans

Potato Gratin

Pinot Noir

Oranges and Pineapple with Orange-Flower Water and Mint
(at left)

Petite Rolled Vanilla Cookies
(page 232)

Strawberry, Mascarpone, and Marsala Parfaits

1   8-ounce container mascarpone cheese*

6   tablespoons sweet Marsala (preferably imported)

3   tablespoons whipping cream

3   tablespoons sugar

3   cups sliced hulled strawberries (about 15 ounces)

2¼   cups coarsely crumbled amaretti cookies (Italian macaroons; about 4½ ounces)*

Combine mascarpone, 3 tablespoons Marsala, cream, and 2 tablespoons sugar in medium bowl. Stir gently until well blended. Combine strawberries, remaining 3 tablespoons Marsala, and 1 tablespoon sugar in another medium bowl; toss to blend. Cover mascarpone and berry mixtures; refrigerate 30 minutes.

Place 2 tablespoons crumbled cookies in each of 6 goblets. Divide strawberry mixture with juices among goblets. Top berries with mascarpone mixture, then remaining cookies. Cover and chill at least 30 minutes and up to 2 hours.

Mascarpone (Italian cream cheese) and amaretti cookies are available at Italian markets and many supermarkets across the country.

6 SERVINGS

Honey-Glazed Grilled Pineapple

½   cup honey

¼   cup fresh lime juice

1   tablespoon grated lime peel

1   teaspoon orange-flower water*

1   large ripe pineapple

¼   cup minced fresh mint

Whisk first 4 ingredients in large glass baking dish. Peel pineapple; cut crosswise into 6 rounds. Remove core; discard. Add pineapple to dish; turn to coat. Cover; let stand at room temperature 1 to 2 hours.

Prepare barbecue (medium heat). Remove pineapple from marinade (reserve marinade). Grill until golden brown, about 3 minutes per side. Transfer to serving dish. Pour reserved marinade over. Sprinkle with mint. Serve warm or chilled.

Available at liquor stores and in the liquor or specialty foods section of supermarkets across the country.

6 SERVINGS

Lemonade Cake with Lemon Glaze

CAKE

Nonstick vegetable oil spray

2¼ cups sifted cake flour

1¾ cups sugar

1 tablespoon baking powder

1 teaspoon salt

½ cup vegetable oil

½ cup lemonade

5 large egg yolks

¼ cup fresh lemon juice

1 tablespoon grated lemon peel

1 cup large egg whites (7 to 8)

½ teaspoon cream of tartar

GLAZE

1 cup (packed) powdered sugar

1 tablespoon fresh lemon juice

½ teaspoon grated lemon peel

1 teaspoon (or more) lemonade

FOR CAKE: Preheat oven to 325°F. Spray 10-inch-diameter tube pan with removable bottom with nonstick spray. Sift flour, sugar, baking powder, and salt into large bowl. Make well in center. Add oil and next 4 ingredients to well. Whisk until smooth. Using electric mixer, beat egg whites and cream of tartar in another large bowl until whites are stiff but not dry. Fold into batter in 4 additions. Pour into pan.

Bake cake until golden and tester inserted near center comes out clean, about 55 minutes. Invert center tube of pan onto narrow-neck bottle; cool cake. *(Can be made 1 day ahead. Turn right side up, cover, and store at room temperature.)*

FOR GLAZE: Whisk sugar, lemon juice, and peel in small bowl until smooth. Add 1 teaspoon lemonade; whisk until glaze has thick, pourable consistency, adding more lemonade by teaspoonfuls, if necessary.

Cut around pan sides; remove sides. Cut cake from bottom of pan. Place right side up on platter. Drizzle with glaze. Let stand 1 hour. *(Can be made 1 day ahead. Cover with cake dome. Store at room temperature.)*

12 SERVINGS

To measure the cake flour, sift some into a large bowl, then measure 2¼ cups.

Vanilla-Citrus Tea Ring

	Nonstick vegetable oil spray
2	cups self-rising flour
1½	cups sugar
1½	tablespoons grated orange peel
1½	tablespoons grated lemon peel
3	large eggs
1	cup extra-light olive oil or vegetable oil
1	cup buttermilk
1	tablespoon vanilla extract

Serve this tender, moist Bundt cake with strawberry compote, vanilla ice cream, or just on its own. Decorate with whole strawberries, if desired.

Preheat oven to 350°F. Generously coat 12-cup Bundt pan with nonstick spray. Whisk flour, sugar, orange peel, and lemon peel in large bowl to blend. Using electric mixer, beat eggs in another large bowl until thick, about 4 minutes. Gradually beat in oil, buttermilk, and vanilla. Add flour mixture and beat until just blended.

Pour batter into prepared pan. Bake cake until tester inserted near center comes out clean, about 45 minutes.

Cool cake in pan on rack 20 minutes. Invert onto platter; cool completely. *(Can be made 1 day ahead. Cover and let stand at room temperature.)*

12 SERVINGS

Warm Apple-Cornmeal Upside-Down Cake

    8 tablespoons (1 stick) unsalted butter, room temperature
  ½ cup plus ¾ cup sugar
 1½ pounds Braeburn or Golden Delicious apples (about 4 medium), peeled, quartered, cored,
       each quarter cut into 2 wedges

  ¾ cup all purpose flour
    2 teaspoons baking powder
  ½ teaspoon salt
  ⅓ cup yellow cornmeal
  ½ cup boiling water
    2 large eggs
    1 teaspoon vanilla extract
  ⅓ cup whole milk

       Vanilla ice cream

Preheat oven to 350°F. Generously butter 9-inch-diameter cake pan with 1½-inch-high sides; line pan with 10-inch-diameter parchment paper round (parchment will come ½ inch up sides of pan). Butter parchment. Melt 2 tablespoons butter in 10-inch-diameter nonstick skillet over medium heat. Add ½ cup sugar and cook until sugar dissolves and mixture turns deep golden brown, stirring occasionally, about 6 minutes. Add apple wedges and gently shake skillet to distribute caramel evenly. Cover and cook until apples release their juices, about 5 minutes. Uncover and cook until apples are tender and caramel thickens and coats apples, stirring occasionally, about 13 minutes. Transfer apples and caramel syrup to prepared cake pan, spreading evenly.

Whisk flour, baking powder, and salt in small bowl to blend. Place cornmeal in large bowl; pour ½ cup boiling water over and stir to blend. Add 6 tablespoons butter and ¾ cup sugar to cornmeal. Using electric mixer, beat until well blended. Beat in eggs and vanilla. Beat in flour mixture alternately with milk in 2 additions each. Pour batter over apples in pan.

Bake cake until golden and tester inserted into center comes out clean, about 40 minutes. Cool cake in pan 5 minutes. Run small knife between cake and pan sides to loosen cake. Carefully invert cake onto ovenproof or microwavable platter and peel off parchment. Cool 15 minutes. (*Cake can be made up to 6 hours ahead. Rewarm in 350°F oven about 10 minutes or microwave on medium just until slightly warm, about 2 minutes.*)

Cut cake into wedges, place on plates, and serve warm with a scoop of vanilla ice cream.

6 TO 8 SERVINGS

Mascarpone Cheesecake with Candied Pecans and Dulce de Leche Sauce

CRUST

8 ounces shortbread cookies

⅓ cup pecans (about 1½ ounces)

2 tablespoons (¼ stick) unsalted butter, melted

FILLING

12 ounces cream cheese, room temperature

2 8-ounce containers mascarpone cheese,* room temperature

1½ tablespoons all purpose flour

1¼ cups sugar

1 teaspoon vanilla extract

½ teaspoon fresh lemon juice

4 large eggs, room temperature

Candied Pecans (see recipe opposite)

Dulce de Leche Sauce (see recipe opposite)

FOR CRUST: Preheat oven to 350°F. Wrap outside of 9-inch-diameter springform pan with 2¾-inch-high sides with 3 layers of heavy-duty foil. Finely grind shortbread cookies and pecans in processor. Add melted butter and process until crumbs are moistened. Press crumb mixture onto bottom (not sides) of prepared pan. Bake crust until golden, about 15 minutes. Cool crust completely on rack. Reduce oven temperature to 325°F.

FOR FILLING: Using electric mixer, beat cream cheese in large bowl until smooth. Add mascarpone and flour; beat until smooth, occasionally scraping down sides of bowl with

rubber spatula. Gradually add sugar and beat until smooth. Beat in vanilla and lemon juice. Add eggs 1 at a time, beating just until blended after each addition.

Pour filling over crust in pan. Place springform pan in large roasting pan. Pour enough hot water into roasting pan to come halfway up sides of springform pan. Bake cheesecake until top is golden and cake is almost set (center 2 inches will still move slightly when pan is gently shaken), about 1 hour 15 minutes. Cool cake on rack 1 hour. Refrigerate uncovered overnight. (*Can be made 2 days ahead. Cover and keep refrigerated.*)

Arrange Candied Pecans decoratively atop cake. Cut cake into wedges. Serve with Dulce de Leche Sauce.

Italian cream cheese, available at Italian markets and many supermarkets.

14 SERVINGS

Dulce de leche is a soft milk-caramel confection that has become one of America's top dessert flavors. If you don't have time to make the sauce, look for it with the ice cream toppings at the market. Note that the baked cheesecake must be chilled overnight before serving.

Candied Pecans

Nonstick vegetable oil spray
½ cup sugar
2 tablespoons water
Pinch of cream of tartar
¾ cup pecan halves (about 3 ounces)

Line baking sheet with foil; spray with nonstick spray. Combine sugar, 2 tablespoons water, and cream of tartar in heavy small saucepan. Stir over medium-low heat until sugar dissolves. Increase heat; boil without stirring until syrup is deep amber color, occasionally brushing down sides of pan with pastry brush dipped in water and swirling pan, about 7 minutes. Remove from heat. Immediately stir in pecans. Quickly pour mixture out onto prepared baking sheet. Working quickly and using 2 forks, separate pecans into individual halves. Cool completely. Break candied pecans apart, leaving each pecan half intact with some candied caramel attached. (*Can be made 1 week ahead. Store airtight at room temperature.*)

MAKES ABOUT 1 CUP

Dulce de Leche Sauce

1 cup whipping cream
1 cup (packed) dark brown sugar
½ cup sweetened condensed milk

Combine whipping cream and brown sugar in heavy medium saucepan. Stir over medium heat until sugar dissolves. Boil until mixture is reduced to 1 cup, stirring occasionally, about 5 minutes. Stir in sweetened condensed milk. (*Can be made 1 day ahead. Cover and chill. Rewarm over medium-low heat just until warm and pourable.*)

MAKES ABOUT 1⅓ CUPS

Gingerbread Cake with Caramelized Pear Compote

CAKE

Nonstick vegetable oil spray
1   15- to 16-ounce can pear halves in syrup, drained well
¾   cup buttermilk
1   tablespoon vanilla extract

3   cups all purpose flour
1½ teaspoons ground cinnamon
1   teaspoon baking soda
¾   teaspoon ground ginger
¾   teaspoon ground allspice
½   teaspoon salt
¼   teaspoon ground cloves
1   cup (2 sticks) unsalted butter, room temperature
1   cup (packed) dark brown sugar
¾   cup mild-flavored (light) molasses
3   large eggs

COMPOTE

¼   cup (½ stick) unsalted butter
2½ pounds Bosc pears, peeled, halved, cored, cut crosswise into ¼-inch-thick slices
½   cup sugar

Vanilla ice cream

FOR CAKE: Preheat oven to 350°F. Spray 12-cup Bundt pan with nonstick spray, then butter and flour pan. Puree canned pears in blender until smooth. Place ¾ cup puree in small bowl for cake (reserve any remaining puree for another use); mix in buttermilk and vanilla.

Sift flour and next 6 ingredients into medium bowl. Using electric mixer, beat butter in large bowl until fluffy. Add brown sugar and beat until blended. Gradually beat in molasses. Beat in eggs 1 at a time (batter may appear curdled). Beat in flour mixture in 3 additions alternately with pear mixture in 2 additions.

Transfer batter to pan. Bake cake until tester inserted near center comes out clean, about 55 minutes. Cool cake in pan on rack 10 minutes. Turn out onto rack; cool completely. *(Can be made 1 day ahead. Cover; let stand at room temperature.)*

FOR COMPOTE: Melt butter in large skillet over high heat. Add pears; sprinkle sugar over. Sauté until pears are tender and juices thicken, stirring often, about 18 minutes. Let stand at room temperature at least 1 hour and up to 4 hours.

Rewarm compote over low heat, stirring gently. Serve cake with compote and ice cream.

8 TO 10 SERVINGS

Bittersweet Molten Chocolate Cakes with Coffee Ice Cream

12 teaspoons plus 5 tablespoons sugar

8 ounces bittersweet (not unsweetened) or semisweet chocolate, chopped

¾ cup (1½ sticks) unsalted butter

3 large eggs

3 large egg yolks

1 tablespoon all purpose flour

1 quart coffee ice cream

For best results, use a dark baking chocolate with high cocoa butter content (about 30 percent), such as Valrhona or Callebaut.

Generously butter eight ¾-cup soufflé dishes or custard cups. Sprinkle inside of each dish with 1½ teaspoons sugar.

Stir chocolate and butter in heavy medium saucepan over low heat until smooth. Remove from heat. Using electric mixer, beat eggs, egg yolks, and remaining 5 tablespoons sugar in large bowl until thick and pale yellow, about 8 minutes. Fold ⅓ of warm chocolate mixture into egg mixture, then fold in remaining chocolate. Fold in flour. Divide batter among soufflé dishes. *(Can be made 1 day ahead. Cover with plastic; chill. Bring to room temperature before continuing.)*

Preheat oven to 425°F. Place soufflé dishes on baking sheet. Bake cakes uncovered until edges are puffed and slightly cracked but 1 inch in center of each moves slightly when dishes are shaken gently, about 13 minutes.

Top each cake with scoop of coffee ice cream and serve immediately.

8 SERVINGS

Brownie Cupcakes with Peanut Butter Frosting

CUPCAKES

- 6 tablespoons (¾ stick) unsalted butter, cut into 4 pieces
- 1¼ cups semisweet chocolate chips (about 8 ounces)
- 3 ounces unsweetened chocolate, chopped
- ½ cup (packed) golden brown sugar
- ⅓ cup sugar
- 2 large eggs
- 1 teaspoon vanilla extract
- ½ cup all purpose flour
- ⅓ cup walnuts, toasted, chopped
- ¼ teaspoon salt

FROSTING

- 1 cup powdered sugar
- ¾ cup creamy peanut butter (do not use old-fashioned or freshly ground)
- ¼ cup (½ stick) unsalted butter, room temperature
- ¼ teaspoon vanilla extract
- 4 teaspoons (about) whipping cream (optional)

  Chocolate shavings or chocolate sprinkles

For kids of all ages, this dessert is dense and chocolaty, and comes in a cute package.

FOR CUPCAKES: Preheat oven to 350°F. Line 10 standard (⅓-cup) muffin cups with paper liners. Combine butter, ½ cup chocolate chips, and unsweetened chocolate in top of double boiler set over simmering water. Stir until mixture is melted and smooth. Remove from over water. Whisk both sugars into chocolate mixture, then whisk in eggs 1 at a time. Whisk in vanilla, then flour, walnuts, salt, and remaining ¾ cup chocolate chips. Divide batter among prepared muffin cups (about ¼ cup for each). Bake cupcakes until tester inserted into center comes out with moist crumbs attached, about 20 minutes. Transfer cupcakes to rack and cool completely.

FOR FROSTING: Put powdered sugar and next 3 ingredients in medium bowl. Using electric mixer, beat until mixture is smooth, adding whipping cream by teaspoonfuls if frosting is too thick to spread.

Spread frosting in swirls over top of cupcakes. Sprinkle with chocolate shavings or chocolate sprinkles. (*Can be made 1 day ahead. Store in single layer in airtight container at room temperature.*)

MAKES 10

Tropical Carrot Cake with Coconut Cream Cheese Frosting

CAKE

2⅓ cups sifted all purpose flour (sifted, then measured)
1 cup sweetened flaked coconut
1 cup dry-roasted macadamia nuts
¾ cup chopped crystallized ginger
3½ teaspoons ground cinnamon
2½ teaspoons baking powder
1 teaspoon salt
½ teaspoon baking soda

2 cups sugar
1 cup vegetable oil
4 large eggs
2 teaspoons vanilla extract
2 cups finely grated peeled carrots
2 8-ounce cans crushed pineapple in its own juice, well drained

FROSTING

3 8-ounce packages Philadelphia-brand cream cheese, room temperature
¾ cup (1½ sticks) unsalted butter, room temperature
2 cups powdered sugar
¾ cup canned sweetened cream of coconut (such as Coco López)
1 teaspoon vanilla extract
½ teaspoon (scant) coconut extract

14 whole dry-roasted macadamia nuts
¼ cup chopped crystallized ginger

FOR CAKE: Preheat oven to 350°F. Butter three 9-inch-diameter cake pans with 1½-inch-high sides. Line bottom of pans with parchment paper. Combine ⅓ cup flour and next 3 ingredients in processor. Process until nuts are finely chopped. Whisk remaining 2 cups flour, cinnamon, baking powder, salt, and baking soda in medium bowl to blend.

Using electric mixer, beat sugar and oil in large bowl to blend. Add eggs 1 at a time, beating well after each addition. Beat in vanilla. Beat in flour-spice mixture. Stir in coconut-macadamia mixture, then carrots and crushed pineapple.

Divide batter among pans. Bake until tester inserted into center of cakes comes out clean, about 30 minutes. Cool in pans on racks 1 hour. Run knife around edge of pans to loosen cakes. Turn cakes out onto racks; cool completely.

FOR FROSTING: Beat cream cheese and butter in large bowl until smooth. Beat in powdered sugar, then cream of coconut and both extracts. Chill until firm enough to spread, about 30 minutes.

Place 1 cake layer, flat side up, on platter. Spread ¾ cup frosting over top of cake. Top with second cake layer, flat side up. Spread ¾ cup frosting over. Top with third cake layer, rounded side up, pressing slightly to adhere. Spread thin layer of frosting over top and sides of cake. Chill cake and remaining frosting 30 minutes. Spread remaining frosting over top and sides of cake. Arrange whole nuts and ginger around top edge of cake. Chill 1 hour. *(Can be made 1 day ahead. Cover with cake dome and chill. Let stand at room temperature 1 hour before serving.)*

8 TO 10 SERVINGS

This cake can be prepared one day ahead. Sweetened cream of coconut is available in the liquor section of most supermarkets.

Pine Nut Torta

3	large egg yolks
1	large egg
1½	teaspoons (packed) grated lemon peel
1	teaspoon vanilla extract
¼	teaspoon salt
10	tablespoons (1¼ sticks) unsalted butter, room temperature
1	cup sugar
1½	cups unbleached all purpose flour
¾	cup pine nuts (about 3½ ounces)
	Powdered sugar

Position rack in center of oven and preheat to 375°F. Butter and flour 10-inch-diameter springform pan. Whisk egg yolks, egg, lemon peel, vanilla, and salt in small bowl to blend. Using electric mixer, beat butter and 1 cup sugar in medium bowl until pale and creamy. Gradually add flour, beating until mixture resembles coarse meal. Using rubber spatula, gently stir egg mixture into butter mixture (batter will be thick). Spoon batter into prepared pan; smooth top (cake will be thin). Sprinkle pine nuts over top; press lightly to adhere.

Bake cake until tester inserted into center comes out clean, about 30 minutes. Transfer cake to rack. Run small knife around cake edges to loosen. Remove pan sides. Cool cake completely. *(Can be made 1 day ahead. Cover and store at room temperature.)*

Sprinkle cake with powdered sugar.

6 TO 8 SERVINGS

Simple and rustic, this deliciously buttery, moist cake is similar in texture to marzipan. Serve with a compote of dried fruit and a bottle of Vin Santo, a Tuscan dessert wine made from dried grapes.

Pecan Molasses Bundt Cake with Bourbon Glaze

CAKE

Nonstick vegetable oil spray

3¼ cups cake flour

2 teaspoons baking powder

¾ teaspoon salt

2 cups sugar

1 cup (2 sticks) unsalted butter, room temperature

4 teaspoons vanilla extract

4 large eggs
1 cup whole milk

1 cup pecans, toasted, finely chopped
¼ cup dark corn syrup
¼ cup mild-flavored (light) molasses
½ teaspoon baking soda

GLAZE
2 teaspoons water
1 teaspoon baking soda
2 cups sugar
1 cup buttermilk
1 cup (2 sticks) unsalted butter
2 teaspoons dark corn syrup
½ cup bourbon
2 teaspoons vanilla extract

FOR CAKE: Preheat oven to 350°F. Spray 10-inch-diameter Bundt pan with nonstick spray; dust with flour. Sift flour, baking powder, and salt into medium bowl. Beat sugar, butter, and 2 teaspoons vanilla in large bowl until fluffy. Beat in eggs 1 at a time. Beat in flour mixture in 3 additions, alternating with milk in 2 additions. Transfer half of batter to prepared pan.

Stir pecans, dark corn syrup, molasses, and 2 teaspoons vanilla extract in another medium bowl to blend. Stir in baking soda. Stir pecan mixture into remaining cake batter in bowl. Spoon pecan batter over batter in pan (do not swirl). Bake until tester inserted near center of cake comes out with dry crumbs attached, about 50 minutes. Transfer cake in pan to rack.

MEANWHILE, PREPARE GLAZE: Stir 2 teaspoons water and baking soda in small bowl to dissolve baking soda. Bring sugar, buttermilk, butter, and corn syrup to boil in heavy 6-quart saucepan over high heat, stirring to dissolve sugar and melt butter. Reduce heat to medium-high. Stir in baking soda mixture (glaze will bubble). Boil until sauce is golden and slightly thickened, stirring often, about 8 minutes. Remove from heat. Stir in bourbon and vanilla.

Invert warm cake onto platter. Immediately brush with 1½ cups hot glaze. Cool completely. *(Can be made 1 day ahead. Cover; let stand at room temperature. Cover; chill remaining glaze.)*

Rewarm remaining glaze. Serve cake with warm glaze.

12 TO 16 SERVINGS

Dessert Buffet for 12

Champagne and
Sparkling Water

Raspberry-Chocolate Tart
(page 183)

**Pecan Molasses Bundt Cake
with Bourbon Glaze**
(opposite; pictured opposite)

**Lemon Curd and
Blueberry Trifle**
(page 210)

**Orange Shortbread Cookies
with Chocolate Chips**
(page 227)

Coffee and *Tea*

Triple-Layer White Cake with
Orange Curd Filling and Frosting

ORANGE CURD

¼ cup fresh lemon juice

2 teaspoons unflavored gelatin

1½ cups sugar

1 cup orange juice

9 large egg yolks

3 tablespoons grated orange peel

2 teaspoons grated lemon peel

¾ cup (1½ sticks) unsalted butter, cut into ½-inch cubes

CAKE

2¾ cups cake flour

1¼ cups plus ⅔ cup sugar

¾ teaspoon baking powder

½ teaspoon salt

¾ cup vegetable oil

4 large egg yolks

6 tablespoons sour cream

½ cup plus 1 tablespoon whole milk

2 teaspoons grated orange peel

1½ teaspoons vanilla extract

6 large egg whites

FROSTING

10 ounces cream cheese, room temperature

10 tablespoons (1¼ sticks) unsalted butter, room temperature

1⅔ cups powdered sugar

FOR ORANGE CURD: Place lemon juice in small bowl or custard cup. Sprinkle gelatin over. Let stand 15 minutes.

Whisk sugar, orange juice, yolks, orange peel, and lemon peel in heavy large saucepan to blend. Add butter. Whisk over medium heat until curd thickens and bubbles begin to appear at edges, about 9 minutes. Remove from heat. Add gelatin mixture. Whisk until gelatin dissolves. Transfer curd to small bowl. Press plastic wrap onto surface of curd. Chill overnight.

FOR CAKE: Preheat oven to 350°F. Butter and flour three 9-inch-diameter cake pans with 1½-inch-high sides. Sift flour, 1¼ cups sugar, baking powder, and salt into medium bowl. Whisk oil and egg yolks in large bowl until well blended. Whisk in sour cream, then milk, orange peel, and vanilla. Whisk in dry ingredients in 3 additions. Using electric mixer, beat

egg whites in another large bowl until soft peaks form. Gradually add remaining ²/₃ cup sugar, beating until whites are stiff but not dry; fold into batter in 4 additions. Divide batter among prepared pans.

Bake cakes until tester inserted into center comes out clean, about 20 minutes. Cool cakes in pans 5 minutes. Cut around pan sides. Turn cakes out onto racks and cool completely.

Place 1 cake layer, flat side up, on 8-inch tart pan bottom or platter. Spread 1 cup curd over. Top with second cake layer, flat side down. Spread 1 cup curd over. Top with third cake layer, flat side down. Cover; refrigerate assembled cake.

FOR FROSTING: Using electric mixer, beat cream cheese and butter in medium bowl until smooth. Beat in powdered sugar, then ³/₄ cup orange curd. Spread frosting over cake. (*Can be made 1 day ahead. Cover with cake dome; refrigerate.*)

10 TO 12 SERVINGS

Chill the orange curd overnight before using.

Buttermilk Panna Cotta with Tropical Fruit

 2   tablespoons water
 2   teaspoons unflavored gelatin

 1   cup whipping cream
 7   tablespoons sugar

 2   cups reduced fat buttermilk (2%)
 ¾   teaspoon vanilla extract

 2   cups ½-inch cubes peeled assorted tropical fruits (such as mango, papaya, and kiwi)

Pour 2 tablespoons water into small custard cup; sprinkle unflavored gelatin over. Let stand until gelatin softens, approximately 10 minutes.

Combine whipping cream and sugar in heavy medium saucepan. Stir over medium heat until sugar dissolves and mixture is hot but not boiling. Remove from heat; add gelatin mixture and stir until gelatin is completely dissolved and mixture is smooth. Cool mixture to room temperature, about 45 minutes.

Stir buttermik and vanilla extract into cream mixture. Pour mixture through fine strainer into 4-cup measuring cup. Divide mixture among six ¾-cup custard cups or ramekins. Refrigerate until panna cotta is set, at least 6 hours and up to 1 day.

Run thin sharp knife around sides of each panna cotta to loosen. One at a time, place bottom of each custard cup in 1 inch of hot water 30 to 45 seconds; immediately invert custard cup onto plate. Using both hands, firmly grasp custard cup and plate together, shaking gently and allowing panna cotta to settle onto plate. Spoon fruit mixture around each panna cotta and serve.

6 SERVINGS

MOUSSES &

PUDDINGS

Bittersweet Chocolate Soufflé with Earl Grey Custard Sauce

SAUCE

- 6 large egg yolks
- 2 tablespoons plus ½ cup sugar
- 1½ cups whole milk
- ½ cup whipping cream
- 1 tablespoon Earl Grey tea leaves (from 3 tea bags)

SOUFFLÉ

- ⅓ cup whole milk
- 8 tablespoons sugar
- 2½ ounces unsweetened chocolate, chopped
- 2½ ounces bittersweet (not unsweetened) or semisweet chocolate, chopped
- 2 large egg yolks
- 5 large egg whites

Be sure to serve the aromatic sauce with each portion of soufflé. The sauce can be prepared one day before the soufflé is made.

FOR SAUCE: Whisk egg yolks and 2 tablespoons sugar in medium bowl to blend well. Combine milk, cream, tea leaves, and remaining ½ cup sugar in heavy medium saucepan. Bring to simmer over medium heat, stirring until sugar dissolves. Gradually whisk hot milk mixture into egg yolk mixture; return to same saucepan. Stir over medium-low heat until custard thickens enough to leave path on spoon when finger is drawn across, about 8 minutes (do not boil). Immediately strain sauce into small bowl. Refrigerate uncovered until cold, at least 4 hours. *(Can be made 1 day ahead. Cover; keep chilled.)*

FOR SOUFFLÉ: Preheat oven to 375°F. Generously butter 6-cup soufflé dish; coat dish with sugar. Combine milk and 5 tablespoons sugar in heavy medium saucepan. Stir over medium-low heat until sugar dissolves and milk comes to simmer. Remove from heat; add both chocolates and stir until melted and smooth. Whisk in egg yolks.

Using electric mixer, beat whites in medium bowl until soft peaks form. Gradually add 3 tablespoons sugar, beating until stiff but not dry. Fold whites into warm chocolate mixture in 3 additions. Transfer mixture to prepared dish.

Bake soufflé until just set in center and top is puffed and cracked all over, about 32 minutes. Serve soufflé immediately with custard sauce.

6 SERVINGS

Lemon Curd and Blueberry Trifle

LEMON CURD

1⅓ cups sugar

¾ cup (1½ sticks) unsalted butter, cut into ½-inch cubes

⅔ cup fresh lemon juice

1 tablespoon grated lemon peel

⅛ teaspoon salt

5 large eggs, beaten to blend

LEMON SYRUP

1 cup water

1 cup sugar

⅓ cup fresh lemon juice

1 tablespoon (packed) grated lemon peel

FILLING

1 8-ounce package cream cheese, room temperature

¾ cup sugar

2¼ cups chilled heavy whipping cream

¼ teaspoon vanilla extract

3 ½-pint containers fresh blueberries

1 12-ounce purchased pound cake, cut into 1-inch cubes

FOR LEMON CURD: Combine first 5 ingredients in heavy medium saucepan. Stir over medium heat until butter melts and sugar dissolves. Remove from heat. Gradually whisk in eggs. Whisk constantly over medium-low heat until curd thickens, about 2 minutes (do not boil). Strain curd through sieve into bowl. Press plastic wrap directly onto surface of curd; refrigerate overnight.

FOR LEMON SYRUP: Combine all ingredients in small saucepan. Bring to boil, stirring until sugar dissolves. Reduce heat and simmer 5 minutes. Cool.

FOR FILLING: Using electric mixer, beat cream cheese, ½ cup sugar, ¼ cup whipping cream, and vanilla extract in large bowl until smooth. Beat 2 cups whipping cream and ¼ cup sugar in another large bowl until peaks form. Fold whipped cream into cream cheese mixture in 2 additions.

Puree 1 container blueberries and ¼ cup lemon syrup in processor. Transfer to medium bowl. Add 1½ containers blueberries and mash with potato masher until chunky puree forms. Reserve remaining blueberries for garnish.

Arrange ⅓ of pound cake cubes (about 2 generous cups) in bottom of 14-cup glass trifle dish. Drizzle with 7 tablespoons lemon syrup. Spoon ⅓ of cream cheese filling (about 2 cups) over cake in dollops; spread to sides of dish. Spoon half of blueberry puree over;

spread to sides of dish. Spoon half of lemon curd (about 1¼ cups) over blueberry puree in dollops, then spread to sides of dish. Repeat layering with ⅓ of cake cubes, 7 tablespoons lemon syrup, ⅓ of cream cheese filling, and remaining blueberry puree, then remaining cake cubes, 7 tablespoons lemon syrup, and remaining lemon curd. Spread remaining cream cheese filling over. Sprinkle with reserved blueberries. Cover and chill overnight. *(Can be made 2 days ahead. Keep refrigerated.)* Spoon trifle into dessert dishes.

10 TO 12 SERVINGS

This luscious dessert can be prepared up to two days before serving. Instead of the traditional custard, whipped cream folded into cream cheese is the easy filling in this version.

Pear Clafouti

5   tablespoons unsalted butter, melted
4   Anjou pears (about 1¾ pounds), peeled, halved, cored, cut
        crosswise into thin slices

4   large eggs
1   cup whole milk
½   cup sugar
6   tablespoons all purpose flour
2   tablespoons brandy
1   teaspoon grated lemon peel
1   teaspoon vanilla extract
¼   teaspoon salt

A *clafouti* is a custardy dessert that's studded with fresh fruit. Purchased cookies are a nice accompaniment.

Preheat oven to 325°F. Generously butter 10-inch-diameter glass pie dish. Heat 1 tablespoon butter in heavy large skillet over medium-high heat. Add pears and sauté until soft and beginning to brown, about 8 minutes. Cool pears in skillet.

Blend eggs and next 7 ingredients in blender until batter is smooth. Add remaining 4 tablespoons butter and blend to combine. Arrange pears in prepared dish. Pour batter over.

Bake clafouti until set and puffed and brown on top, about 55 minutes. Cool at least 15 minutes. Serve clafouti warm or at room temperature.

8 TO 10 SERVINGS

Rice Pudding with Raisins and Cinnamon

6 cups water
2 cups long-grain white rice

6 2x½-inch strips lemon peel (yellow part only)
½ teaspoon salt

5 cups (or more) whole milk
1 cup sweetened condensed milk
1 cup evaporated milk
2 cinnamon sticks
2 vanilla beans, split lengthwise in half
¾ cup brown raisins or golden raisins
2 tablespoons sugar

Ground cinnamon
Grated peel from 1 lemon
Additional cinnamon sticks (optional)

Bring 2 cups water to boil in medium saucepan. Remove from heat. Add rice; let stand 15 minutes. Pour rice into strainer and drain, then rinse rice under cold running water until water runs clear.

Bring 4 cups water to boil in large saucepan. Add rice, lemon peel strips, and salt and return to boil. Reduce heat to low, cover, and simmer until rice is almost tender, about 10 minutes. Drain. Discard lemon peel.

Combine 5 cups milk, sweetened condensed milk, evaporated milk, and 2 cinnamon sticks in heavy large saucepan. Scrape in seeds from vanilla beans; add beans. Bring to boil. Reduce heat to medium and boil gently until mixture thickens and is reduced to 2¾ cups, about 30 minutes. Stir in rice, raisins, and sugar. Stir until raisins are plump and flavors blend, about 5 minutes.

Spoon pudding into bowls. Sprinkle with ground cinnamon and grated lemon peel. Garnish with cinnamon sticks, if desired.

8 TO 10 SERVINGS

Pear Charlottes with Chamomile Crème Anglaise

RAISINS AND PEARS

½ cup water

¼ cup sugar

¾ cup golden raisins

¼ cup dark rum

3 tablespoons honey

1¾ pounds firm but ripe Bartlett pears (about 4 medium), peeled, cored,
cut into ½-inch cubes

CUSTARDS

2 16-ounce brioche or egg bread loaves, crusts trimmed, bread cut into ⅓-inch-thick slices

1⅓ cups heavy whipping cream

6 tablespoons sugar

3 large eggs

2 tablespoons dark rum

2 teaspoons vanilla extract

Chamomile Crème Anglaise (see recipe opposite)

FOR RAISINS AND PEARS: Bring ½ cup water and sugar to boil in heavy small saucepan, stirring until sugar dissolves. Remove from heat. Mix in golden raisins and dark rum. Let soak 1 hour. Drain raisins.

Meanwhile, heat honey in large nonstick skillet over medium heat. Add pears; sauté just until tender, about 2 minutes. Cool. Mix in raisins.

FOR CUSTARDS: Preheat oven to 350°F. Butter eight 1¼-cup custard cups, then sprinkle with sugar. Place cups on baking sheet. Place 8 bread slices on work surface. Cut out 1 round from each slice to fit cup bottoms. Line cup bottoms with bread rounds. Cut enough of remaining bread slices into strips wide enough to line cup sides; line cup sides completely with strips, cutting to fit. Cut enough of remaining bread into ½-inch cubes to measure 4 cups.

Whisk cream, sugar, eggs, rum, and vanilla in large bowl to blend well. Add 4 cups bread cubes and fruit mixture; stir to blend. Divide among prepared cups.

Bake charlottes until center is puffed and set, about 55 minutes. (*Can be made 2 hours ahead. Let stand at room temperature. Warm in 350°F oven for 7 minutes.*) Run knife around sides of charlottes. Invert onto plates. Spoon crème anglaise over warm charlottes.

MAKES 8

Chamomile Crème Anglaise

2½ cups half and half
  8 chamomile tea bags

  8 large egg yolks
⅓ cup sugar

Bring half and half to simmer in heavy medium saucepan. Add tea bags; remove from heat. Cover; let steep 30 minutes. Strain mixture through strainer into bowl; discard tea bags. Return half and half to same saucepan; bring to simmer.

Whisk yolks and sugar in medium bowl to blend. Gradually whisk in hot half and half. Return to same saucepan. Stir over medium-low heat until sauce thickens very slightly, about 15 minutes (do not boil; sauce will be thin but will thicken slightly when cold). Cover and chill overnight. *(Can be made 2 days ahead. Keep chilled.)* Serve cold.

MAKES ABOUT 2 CUPS

Coffee-Cardamom Flans with Orange Crème Fraîche

2 cups sugar
⅓ cup water
1 teaspoon light corn syrup

4 cups whole milk
¼ cup finely ground espresso beans
1 tablespoon whole green cardamom pods, each cracked slightly

6 large egg yolks
2 large eggs

Orange Crème Fraîche (see recipe below)

Stir 1 cup sugar, ⅓ cup water, and corn syrup in heavy medium saucepan over low heat until sugar dissolves. Increase heat and boil without stirring until caramel is deep amber color, brushing down sides of pan with wet pastry brush and swirling pan occasionally, about 7 minutes. Working quickly, pour caramel into eight ¾-cup custard cups. Tilt and rotate each cup to coat sides and bottom.

Stir milk, ground coffee, cardamom, and ½ cup sugar in heavy medium saucepan over medium heat until sugar dissolves and mixture simmers. Remove pan from heat; let mixture steep 1 hour.

Preheat oven to 350°F. Whisk egg yolks, whole eggs, and remaining ½ cup sugar in large bowl to blend. Return milk mixture to simmer; gradually whisk into egg mixture. Line sieve with several layers of moistened cheesecloth; strain custard into bowl, then divide among caramel-lined cups. Arrange cups in 13x9x2-inch metal baking pan. Pour enough hot water into baking pan to come halfway up sides of cups. Cover pan loosely with foil.

Bake flans 20 minutes. Lift foil to allow steam to escape. Replace foil. Bake flans until softly set in center, lifting foil every 10 minutes, about 35 minutes longer. Remove flans from water. Chill flans 4 hours; cover and chill overnight.

Run knife around flans. Turn out onto plates. Serve with crème fraîche.

8 SERVINGS

Orange Crème Fraîche

½ cup whipping cream
1 tablespoon grated orange peel
½ cup crème fraîche*
1 tablespoon sugar

Bring cream and orange peel to simmer in heavy small saucepan over medium heat. Pour into medium bowl. Place bowl inside large bowl of ice water to chill quickly. Whisk in crème fraîche. Chill until mixture is very cold, at least 1 hour. Add sugar and whisk until firm peaks form. Cover and chill up to 3 hours. Rewhip, if necessary.

Sold at some supermarkets. If unavailable, heat 1/2 cup whipping cream to lukewarm (85°F). Remove from heat and mix in 1 tablespoon buttermilk. Cover and let stand in warm draft-free area until slightly thickened, 24 to 48 hours, depending on temperature of room. Cover and refrigerate up to 2 days.

MAKES ABOUT 2 CUPS

Crème Brûlée with Berries

1½ cups whipping cream
1 vanilla bean, split lengthwise
9 large egg yolks
½ cup plus 6 teaspoons sugar

2 cups mixed berries (such as raspberries, blueberries, and sliced strawberries)
2 tablespoons (packed) golden brown sugar
1 tablespoon raspberry liqueur (optional)

Preheat oven to 325°F. Place cream in heavy medium saucepan. Scrape in seeds from vanilla bean; add bean. Bring to simmer over medium heat. Whisk yolks and 1/2 cup sugar in medium metal bowl to blend. Set bowl over saucepan of simmering water (do not allow bowl to touch water). Whisk vigorously until yolk mixture is pale yellow and hot to touch, about 3 minutes. Gradually whisk in hot cream mixture; discard vanilla bean.

Divide cream mixture among six 3/4-cup soufflé dishes or custard cups. Arrange dishes in 13x9x2-inch baking pan. Pour enough hot water into pan to come halfway up sides of dishes. Bake custards until almost set in center and light golden on top, about 35 minutes. Remove custards from water; refrigerate overnight.

Preheat broiler. Sprinkle 1 teaspoon sugar atop each custard. Place dishes on small baking sheet. Broil until sugar just starts to caramelize, rotating sheet for even browning, about 2 minutes. Refrigerate custards until topping hardens, at least 30 minutes and up to 3 hours.

Meanwhile, toss berries, brown sugar, and liqueur, if desired, in large bowl. Spoon berry mixture atop custards and serve immediately.

6 SERVINGS

Bistro Dinner for 6

Leek, Potato, and
Tarragon Soup
(page 34)

Pork Chops with
Mustard-Cornichon Sauce
(page 71)

Frisée Salad

Burgundy

Crème Brûlée with Berries
(at left)

Margarita Ice Pops

- ½ cup tequila
- 6 tablespoons fresh lime juice
- ¼ cup coarse kosher salt
- 6 frozen lime-flavored ice pops or fruit bars, unwrapped

Mix tequila and lime juice in 1-cup measuring cup. Place coarse salt in small bowl. Place all ice pops, sticks up, in deep bowl, or place 1 pop in each of 6 glasses. Pour tequila mixture over ice pops. Lightly dip 1 edge of each ice pop into coarse salt and serve.

6 SERVINGS

Double Banana Split with Rum Whipped Cream

- 4 bananas, peeled, split lengthwise
- 8 teaspoons plus ¼ cup (packed) dark brown sugar

- 1 cup chilled whipping cream
- 2 tablespoons dark rum

- 4 slices purchased banana bread, toasted
- 4 scoops vanilla ice cream
- 4 scoops chocolate ice cream
- 4 scoops chocolate chip cookie dough ice cream
- 1 cup pecans, toasted
  Purchased chocolate syrup
  Sweetened flaked coconut, toasted

Preheat broiler. Place banana halves, cut side up, on baking sheet. Sprinkle each with 1 teaspoon sugar. Broil bananas until sugar melts and darkens, about 2 minutes. Set aside.

Using electric mixer, beat whipping cream, dark rum, and remaining ¼ cup sugar in large bowl until peaks form.

Place 1 slice banana bread in each of 4 banana split dishes. Place 1 banana half on each side of bread, parallel to long sides of dish. Top bread with 1 scoop of each ice cream. Sprinkle with pecans and drizzle with chocolate syrup. Top bananas with dollop of rum-whipped cream and sprinkle of coconut.

FROZEN

DESSERTS

4 SERVINGS

Caramelized Pineapple Sundaes
with Chocolate-Coconut Sauce

PRALINE

¾ cup sugar

¼ cup water

½ cup unsalted macadamia nuts,
   coarsely chopped

SAUCE

1 15-ounce can sweetened cream of
   coconut (such as Coco López)

6 tablespoons unsweetened
   cocoa powder

½ teaspoon vanilla extract

½ teaspoon coconut extract
   Pinch of salt

PINEAPPLE

3 tablespoons unsalted butter

2 tablespoons (firmly packed) golden
   brown sugar

1 small pineapple, peeled, cored, cut into 1-inch pieces

2 pints vanilla ice cream

FOR PRALINE: Line 8x8-inch baking pan with foil. Stir sugar and water in heavy small saucepan over medium-low heat until sugar dissolves. Increase heat and boil without stirring until syrup is deep amber color, occasionally brushing down sides of pan with wet pastry brush and swirling pan, about 7 minutes. Mix in nuts. Immediately pour mixture into prepared pan, spreading slightly. Cool completely. Peel foil off praline. Coarsely chop praline. (*Can be made 1 week ahead. Store refrigerated in airtight container.*)

FOR SAUCE: Bring cream of coconut and cocoa to simmer in medium saucepan over medium-low heat, whisking until smooth. Remove from heat. Add extracts and salt; whisk to blend. Cool. (*Can be made 1 day ahead. Cover and chill. Bring to room temperature before using.*)

FOR PINEAPPLE: Melt butter and sugar in very large skillet over medium heat, stirring until sugar dissolves. Increase heat to high. Add pineapple and sauté until golden, about 3 minutes per side. Divide pineapple among 8 sundae dishes. Top each with 1 scoop of ice cream. Top with sauce and praline.

8 SERVINGS

Fresh Strawberry Sorbet

2 cups water
1 cup sugar

1 quart strawberries, hulled
⅓ cup fresh orange juice
⅓ cup fresh lemon juice

Stir 2 cups water and sugar in heavy medium saucepan over high heat until sugar dissolves. Boil 5 minutes.

Working in batches, puree strawberries in food processor until smooth. Add strawberry puree and orange and lemon juices to sugar syrup; stir to blend. Cover and refrigerate until cold, about 2 hours.

Process strawberry mixture in ice cream maker according to manufacturer's instructions or place mixture in shallow container and freeze, stirring every hour until set, about 6 hours. (*Can be made 3 days ahead. Cover and freeze in airtight container. If sorbet is frozen solid, place in refrigerator for 15 minutes to soften.*)

6 SERVINGS

**Lunch on the Lawn
for 6**

Vegetable and
Goat Cheese Tart
(page 108)

Mixed Green Salad

Iced Tea and *Sparkling Water*

Strawberry Sorbet

Butter Cookies

Sorbet and Ice Cream Terrine
with Blackberry Compote

TERRINE

- 1 pint raspberry sorbet
- 1 pint lemon sorbet
- 1 pint vanilla ice cream
- 1 pint mango sorbet
- 1 pint boysenberry sorbet

COMPOTE

- ½ cup seedless blackberry jam
- 2 teaspoons grated lemon peel
- 1 teaspoon fresh lemon juice
- 2 ½-pint containers fresh blackberries
- 1 tablespoon thinly sliced fresh mint leaves

FOR TERRINE: Line 9x5x2¾-inch metal loaf pan with 2 layers of plastic wrap, extending 3 inches over sides. Scoop raspberry sorbet into medium bowl and stir to soften; let stand at room temperature until sorbet is spreadable, stirring occasionally, about 10 minutes. Spread sorbet evenly in bottom of prepared loaf pan. Place loaf pan in freezer. Scoop lemon sorbet into another medium bowl; stir and let stand at room temperature until spreadable, stirring occasionally, about 10 minutes. Spoon lemon sorbet in large dollops

atop raspberry sorbet, then spread in even layer. Return loaf pan to freezer. Repeat procedure with vanilla ice cream, then mango sorbet, and finally boysenberry sorbet. Fold plastic wrap overhang over terrine; cover with aluminum foil. Freeze terrine overnight. (*Terrine can be made 4 days ahead. Keep frozen.*)

FOR COMPOTE: Stir blackberry jam in heavy medium saucepan over medium-low heat until melted. Stir in grated lemon peel and fresh lemon juice. Cool to room temperature. Stir in fresh blackberries, crushing some with fork to release juices. Refrigerate compote until cold, at least 2 hours and up to 1 day.

Stir mint into blackberry compote. Invert terrine onto platter; peel off plastic wrap. Cut terrine into slices. Serve with compote.

10 SERVINGS

A rainbow of four purchased sorbets plus vanilla ice cream make this beauty one of the easiest desserts ever. Prepare the stunning terrine up to four days ahead.

Blackberry Sorbet

1¼ cups sugar

1 cup water

1½ pounds frozen unsweetened blackberries, thawed, juices reserved

2 tablespoons fresh lemon juice

½ small watermelon

16 fresh blackberries

Stir sugar and 1 cup water in small saucepan. Bring to boil over high heat, stirring until sugar dissolves. Boil 1 minute. Transfer syrup to large bowl. Chill until syrup is cold, about 3 hours.

Working in batches, puree blackberries with juices and cold syrup in blender until smooth. Strain into another large bowl; discard seeds. Stir in lemon juice.

Process berry mixture in ice cream maker according to manufacturer's instructions. Transfer sorbet to container; cover and freeze until firm, about 6 hours. (*Can be made 1 week ahead. Keep frozen.*)

Using large spoon, scoop out flesh from watermelon, leaving rind intact and forming bowl (reserve melon for another use or serve alongside sorbet, if desired). Drain excess juice from watermelon bowl. Cover and chill watermelon bowl until cold.

Scoop sorbet into watermelon bowl. Garnish with fresh blackberries.

8 SERVINGS

S'mores Ice Cream Pie with Warm Milk Chocolate Sauce

CRUST

Nonstick vegetable oil spray

1½ cups graham cracker crumbs

6 tablespoons (¾ stick) unsalted butter, melted

FILLING

1 quart chocolate ice cream, slightly softened until spreadable

2 cups coarsely chopped chocolate-covered graham crackers

1½ cups marshmallow creme

2 cups mini marshmallows

SAUCE

½ cup whipping cream

5 ounces imported milk chocolate, finely chopped

FOR CRUST: Preheat oven to 350°F. Spray 9-inch-diameter metal pie pan with nonstick spray. Mix graham cracker crumbs and melted butter in bowl to blend. Transfer to prepared pie pan. Press crumb mixture onto bottom and up sides of pan. Bake until crust is set and golden, about 11 minutes. Cool completely.

FOR FILLING: Using offset spatula, spread half of softened ice cream evenly in crust. Sprinkle 1 cup chopped chocolate-covered graham crackers evenly over. Spread remaining ice cream over, covering graham crackers completely. Freeze until firm, at least 4 hours.

Drop marshmallow creme by tablespoonfuls over top of pie. Using moistened fingertips, spread in even layer, covering top of pie completely. Sprinkle mini marshmallows evenly over, pressing slightly to adhere. Cover and freeze until firm, about 4 hours.

FOR SAUCE: Bring whipping cream to boil in heavy small saucepan. Remove from heat. Add chocolate; let stand 2 minutes to soften, then whisk until melted and smooth. (*Pie and sauce can be made 3 days ahead. Keep pie frozen. Cover and chill sauce; rewarm sauce over low heat just until pourable before serving.*)

Preheat broiler. Cover pie crust edges with foil collar. Broil pie just until marshmallows are golden brown, watching closely to avoid burning and rotating pan to brown evenly if necessary, about 2 minutes. Transfer pie to platter and serve immediately with warm sauce.

8 SERVINGS

Gingered Peach Sundaes

  1 cup chopped dried pitted peaches
  1 cup amaretto liqueur
 ½ cup water
 ¼ cup sugar
1½ tablespoons minced fresh ginger
  2 whole star anise*

  2 pints vanilla ice cream
  2 tablespoons pine nuts, toasted

The ginger-spiced peach sauce for this dessert can be prepared one day before serving.

Combine first 6 ingredients in heavy medium saucepan. Bring to boil over high heat, stirring until sugar dissolves. Reduce heat to low, cover partially, and simmer gently until peaches are tender, about 15 minutes. Cool completely in saucepan. Discard star anise. (*Sauce can be made 1 day ahead. Cover and refrigerate. Bring to room temperature before using.*)

Scoop ice cream into dessert goblets. Spoon peach sauce over; sprinkle with pine nuts and serve immediately.

Brown star-shaped seedpods, available at Asian markets and specialty foods stores and in the spice section of some supermarkets.

6 SERVINGS

Almond Crunch Cookies

3	cups slivered almonds, toasted
1¼	cups powdered sugar
3	large egg whites
1½	cups all purpose flour
1	teaspoon baking soda
½	teaspoon salt
1	cup (2 sticks) unsalted butter, room temperature
¾	cup sugar
3	tablespoons amaretto liqueur
1	teaspoon vanilla extract

Preheat oven to 350°F. Line heavy large baking sheet with parchment paper. Place 1½ cups almonds in large bowl and sift ½ cup powdered sugar over; toss to coat. Whisk 1 egg white to blend in small bowl. Add 1 tablespoon egg white to nuts and toss to blend. Spread mixture in even layer over prepared baking sheet. Bake until almonds are golden and coating is dry, about 10 minutes. Cool completely.

Transfer almonds to processor. Using on/off turns, process until almost all nuts are coarsely chopped and some fine crumbs form. Transfer to small bowl.

Line 2 large baking sheets with parchment paper. Finely chop remaining 1½ cups slivered almonds in processor. Add flour, baking soda, and salt. Blend until nuts are very finely ground.

Using electric mixer, beat butter, ¾ cup sugar, and remaining ¾ cup powdered sugar in large bowl until well blended. Add remaining 2 egg whites, amaretto, and vanilla. Beat until well blended. Gradually mix in flour-almond mixture. Stir in chopped candied almonds.

Working in 2 batches and using small ice cream scoop or table-spoon, spoon 2 level tablespoonfuls dough in mound for each cookie, forming about 12 mounds on each sheet and spacing 2 inches apart. Bake until cookies are golden brown, about 14 minutes. Cool slightly on baking sheets. Transfer cookies to rack and cool completely. *(Can be made 3 days ahead. Store airtight at room temperature.)*

MAKES ABOUT 4 DOZEN

For soft and chewy cookies, bake each batch just a couple of minutes less than the recipe directs.

Orange Shortbread Cookies with Chocolate Chips

- 1½ cups all purpose flour
- ½ teaspoon baking powder
- ½ teaspoon salt
- ½ cup (1 stick) unsalted butter, room temperature
- ½ cup sugar
- 2 teaspoons (packed) grated orange peel
- ½ teaspoon orange extract
- 1 large egg yolk
- 3 tablespoons whipping cream
- 8 ounces double chocolate chips (such as Ghirardelli)

Position rack in center of oven; preheat to 350°F. Butter and flour large baking sheet. Whisk first 3 ingredients in medium bowl. Beat butter, sugar, orange peel, and orange extract in large bowl until fluffy. Beat in yolk, then cream. Add flour mixture; beat until dough comes together in moist clumps. Stir in chocolate chips.

Drop dough by generous tablespoonfuls onto baking sheet, spacing ¾ inch apart. Using moistened fingertips, flatten each to ½-inch-thick round. Bake cookies until golden, about 18 minutes. Transfer to rack; cool. *(Can be made 3 days ahead. Store airtight at room temperature.)*

MAKES ABOUT 20

This recipe calls for double chocolate chips, which have a deep, rich chocolate flavor because they are made with bittersweet chocolate. Regular semisweet chocolate chips can be substituted.

Mexican Wedding Cookies

1 cup (2 sticks) butter, room temperature

2 cups powdered sugar

2 teaspoons vanilla extract

2 cups all purpose flour

1 cup pecans, toasted, coarsely ground

⅛ teaspoon ground cinnamon

Using electric mixer, beat butter in large bowl until light and fluffy. Add ½ cup powdered sugar and vanilla; beat until well blended. Beat in flour, then pecans. Divide dough in half; form each half into ball. Wrap separately in plastic; chill until cold, about 30 minutes.

Preheat oven to 350°F. Whisk remaining 1½ cups powdered sugar and cinnamon in pie dish to blend. Set cinnamon sugar aside.

Working with half of chilled dough, roll dough by 2 teaspoonfuls between palms into balls. Arrange balls on heavy large baking sheet, spacing ½ inch apart. Bake cookies until golden brown on bottom and just pale golden on top, about 18 minutes. Cool cookies 5 minutes on baking sheet. Gently toss warm cookies in cinnamon sugar to coat completely. Transfer coated cookies to rack and cool completely. Repeat procedure with remaining half of dough. (*Cookies can be prepared 2 days ahead. Store airtight at room temperature; reserve remaining cinnamon sugar.*)

Sift remaining cinnamon sugar over cookies and serve.

MAKES ABOUT 4 DOZEN

Turtle Bars

 2 cups all purpose flour

1¾ cups (packed) dark brown sugar

1½ cups (3 sticks) unsalted butter, room temperature

 3 tablespoons whipping cream

 1 cup pecan halves, toasted

 ¾ cup semisweet chocolate chips (about 5½ ounces)

Dark brown sugar gives these buttery treats an extra-rich taste.

Preheat oven to 350°F. Mix flour, 1 cup brown sugar, and ¾ cup butter in processor until well blended and crumbly. Press mixture evenly into ungreased 9x13x2-inch metal baking dish. Bake until crust is light golden, about 15 minutes. Maintain oven temperature.

Meanwhile, bring remaining ¾ cup brown sugar, ¾ cup butter, and cream to boil in small saucepan over high heat, stirring until sugar dissolves. Boil 1 minute, stirring occasionally. Remove caramel from heat.

Sprinkle pecans over crust. Pour caramel over pecans. Bake until bubbles form and color darkens, about 20 minutes. Remove from oven and sprinkle with chocolate chips. Let stand until chocolate chips melt, about 5 minutes. Using offset spatula, spread chocolate over top. Refrigerate bars until chocolate sets, about 20 minutes. Cut into 1-inch squares.

MAKES ABOUT 70

Chocolate-Nut Biscotti

2 cups plus 2 tablespoons all purpose flour
1½ teaspoons baking powder
¼ teaspoon salt
¾ cup sugar
½ cup (1 stick) unsalted butter, room temperature
2 large eggs
2 tablespoons Grand Marnier or other orange liqueur
1 tablespoon grated orange peel
1 cup pecans, lightly toasted, coarsely chopped
6 ounces bittersweet (not unsweetened) chocolate, chopped

Line large baking sheet with parchment paper. Whisk flour, baking powder, and salt in medium bowl to blend. Using electric mixer, beat sugar and butter in large bowl to blend. Beat in eggs 1 at a time, then Grand Marnier and orange peel. Add flour mixture and beat until blended. Stir in pecans and chocolate. Gather dough together; divide in half. Wrap in plastic and freeze 20 minutes to firm.

Position rack in center of oven; preheat to 350°F. Using floured hands, form each dough piece into 14-inch-long, 2½-inch-wide log. Transfer logs to prepared baking sheet, spacing 2 inches apart. Bake until light golden, about 30 minutes. Transfer parchment with logs to rack. Cool 20 minutes. Reduce oven temperature to 300°F.

Place 1 log on cutting board. Using serrated knife, cut log on diagonal into ½-inch-thick slices. Stand slices upright on baking sheet. Repeat with remaining log.

Bake biscotti until dry to touch and pale golden, about 30 minutes. Cool completely on rack. *(Can be made 1 week ahead. Store in airtight container.)*

MAKES ABOUT 3 DOZEN

Oatmeal Cookies with Raisins, Dates, and Walnuts

2 cups all purpose flour
1 teaspoon baking powder
1 teaspoon ground cinnamon
½ teaspoon baking soda
½ teaspoon salt

¾ cup (1½ sticks) unsalted butter, room temperature
¼ cup solid vegetable shortening, room temperature
1 cup sugar
1 cup (packed) dark brown sugar
¼ cup honey
2 large eggs
1 tablespoon vanilla extract
3 cups old-fashioned oats
1 cup raisins
1 cup chopped pitted dates
1 cup chopped walnuts

Preheat oven to 350°F. Line 2 baking sheets with foil; butter foil. Blend first 5 ingredients in medium bowl.

Using electric mixer, beat butter, vegetable shortening, and both sugars in large bowl until fluffy. Beat in honey, eggs, and vanilla. Gradually beat in flour mixture. Stir in oats, raisins, dates, and walnuts. Drop batter by tablespoonfuls onto prepared sheets, spacing mounds 2 inches apart. Flatten cookies slightly.

Bake cookies until golden brown, about 10 minutes. Cool completely on sheets. (*Can be made 2 days ahead. Store airtight at room temperature.*)

MAKES ABOUT 4 DOZEN

Petite Rolled Vanilla Cookies

   5 tablespoons unsalted butter, room temperature
   1 cup powdered sugar
   2 large egg whites
   ½ teaspoon vanilla extract
   ½ cup all purpose flour

Using electric mixer, beat 3 tablespoons butter and sugar in medium bowl until coarse meal forms. Beat in egg whites 1 at a time, then vanilla. Add flour and beat until well blended. Melt 2 tablespoons butter in small saucepan over low heat. Mix warm butter into batter.

Position rack in center of oven and preheat to 350°F. Lightly butter 2 nonstick baking sheets. Spoon 1 heaping teaspoonful batter for each cookie onto sheets, spacing 4 inches apart and forming 3 cookies on each sheet. Using small metal offset spatula or back of spoon, spread batter for each cookie to very thin 4-inch round. Bake cookies on 1 sheet until ¾ inch of edge is golden brown, about 5 minutes. Run thin flexible spatula under edge of 1 cookie to loosen and remove from sheet. Working quickly while cookies are still warm and flexible, roll 1 cookie around handle of wooden spoon into cylinder. Slide cookie onto work surface. Shape remaining cookies into cylinders, returning sheet to oven briefly to soften cookies if necessary.

Bake cookies on second sheet while first baking sheet cools. Repeat with remaining batter, using cool baking sheet each time. Cool rolled cookies completely. *(Can be made 1 day ahead. Store airtight at room temperature).*

MAKES ABOUT 2 DOZEN

Maple-Pecan Sticky Bars

CRUST
   ½ cup (1 stick) unsalted butter, room temperature
   ¼ cup sugar
   1 large egg yolk
  1½ cups all purpose flour
   ⅛ teaspoon salt

FILLING
   ½ cup pure maple syrup
   ⅓ cup (packed) golden brown sugar
   ¼ cup whipping cream
   3 tablespoons unsalted butter
   ½ teaspoon vanilla extract
  1½ cups coarsely chopped pecans

FOR CRUST: Preheat oven to 350°F. Butter 9x9x2-inch metal cake pan. Using electric mixer, beat butter, sugar, and egg yolk in bowl to blend. Add flour and salt; beat until moist clumps form. Gather dough together. Press dough over bottom and ¹/₂ inch up sides of pan. Bake crust until golden, about 20 minutes. Cool.

FOR FILLING: Combine first 4 ingredients in medium saucepan. Bring to boil, stirring until butter melts and mixture is smooth. Boil filling 30 seconds. Remove from heat; mix in vanilla, then nuts.

Pour hot filling into crust. Bake bars until filling is bubbling in center, about 15 minutes. Cool bars completely in pan on rack (filling will become firm). Chill at least 1 hour and up to 2 hours. *(Can be made 3 days ahead. Cover and keep chilled.)* Cut into bars.

MAKES 30

To get a neater slice, chill the bars first.

Index

Page numbers in *italics* indicate color photographs.

Acknowledgments

RECIPES

Bruce Aidells
Elizabeth and Susan Allen
Amy's Bread, New York, New York
John Ash
Michelle and David Bach
Barbara and Bob Bailey
Melanie Barnard
Carole Bloom
Blue Onion Bistro, Seattle, Washington
Daniel Boulud
Bump & Grind Cafe, Denver, Colorado
Jonathan Burrows
Kenny Callaghan
Lauren Chattman
Ann Colton
Colin Cowie
Lane Crowther
Lori De Mori
Sara Dickerman
Brooke Dojny
Eiffel Tower Restaurant, Paris Las Vegas, Las Vegas, Nevada
Jane and Sandy Elliott
Susan Feniger
Barbara Pool Fenzl

Claudia Fleming
Janet Fletcher
Ana Garcia
Genoa, Portland, Oregon
Dorie Greenspan
Debbie Gold
Rozanne Gold
Joyce Goldstein
Carlene and Rosendo Gutierrez
Ken Haedrich
Charmaine Haravey
Heidi and Ron Johnson
Michele Anna Jordan
Terry and Peter Kagan
Jeanne Thiel Kelley
Kendrick's, Christiansted, St. Croix, Virgin Islands
Alex Lee
Susan Herrmann Loomis
Ludovic Lefebvre, Ludo, Santa Monica, California
Amy Stafford Malik
John Malik
Jane and John Marks
Janet Taylor McCracken
Betsy McNair
James McNair
Tory McPhail, Commander's Palace, New Orleans, Louisiana

Tracey Medeiros
Jean François Méteigner, La Cachette, Los Angeles, California
Mary Sue Milliken
Cindy Mushet
Antoinette Muto
Micol Negrin
Cindy Pawlcyn
François Payard
Jamie Purviance
Patricia Quintana
Victoria Abbott Riccardi
Tori Ritchie
Rick Rodgers
Betty Rosbottom
Judy and Robbie Ross
Felino Samson
Roberto Santibañez
Chris Schlesinger
Arthur Schwartz
Sarah Patterson Scott
Nancy Silverton
Marie Simmons
Susan Simon
B. Smith
Michael Smith
Marilyn Tausend
Sarah Tenaglia

Trattoria Garga, Florence, Italy
Juana Vázquez-Gómez
Robb Walsh
John Willingham
Dede Wilson
Patricia Yeo
Nancy Zaslavsky
Ricardo Muñoz Zurita

PHOTOGRAPHY

Noel Barnhurst
John Blais
Wyatt Counts
Fran Gealer
Jacqueline Hopkins
Brian Leatart
Ericka McConnell
William Meppem
Pornchai Mittongtare
Gary Moss
Raymond Patrick
Scott Peterson
David Prince
Lisa Rutledge
Rick Szczechowski
Mark Thomas